EERIE APPALACHIA

Eerie APPALACHIA

SMILING MAN, INDRID COLD, THE JERSEY DEVIL, THE LEGEND OF MOTHMAN AND MORE

Mark Muncy and Kari Schultz

THE
History
PRESS

Published by The History Press
Charleston, SC
www.historypress.com

Front cover: The Appalachians are the home of many monsters and legends. The great Mishipeshu lies in all the waters along the mountains. *Illustration by Kari Schultz. Back cover*: The Mothman flies high over Big Stone Gap, the gateway to the Appalachians. *Photo by Mark Muncy; Mothman illustration by Kari Schultz.*

First published 2022

Manufactured in the United States

ISBN 9781467148184

Library of Congress Control Number: 2022933419

Big Stone Gap at Sunset. The gateway of the Appalachians. *Photo by the author.*

CONTENTS

Acknowledgements   9
Introduction   11

PART I. THE APPALACHIAN TRIANGLE, 1950s and 1960s
Indrid Cold (Parkersburg, West Virginia)   15
The Mothman (Point Pleasant, West Virginia)   19
The Grafton Monster (Grafton, West Virginia)   27
The Hopkinsville Goblins (Kelly, Kentucky)   30
The Loveland Frogmen (Loveland, Ohio)   34
The Flatwoods Monster (Flatwoods, West Virginia)   38

PART II. PRE-1900
Wizard Clip (Middleway, West Virginia)   47
Serpent Mound, Alligator Mound and the Crosswick Serpent
   (Ohio River Valley)   51

PART III. HAUNTED HOT SPOTS
The Kirkbride Asylums: Trans-Allegheny, Waverly Hills,
   Penhurst and the Ridges (Weston, West Virginia;
   Louisville, Kentucky; Spring City, Pennsylvania;
   and Athens, Ohio)   59
Screaming Jenny (Moulton, Alabama)   66
The Moonville Tunnel (Vinton County, Ohio)   68
The Greenbriar Ghost (Lewisburg, West Virginia)   70

CONTENTS

PART IV. EVERY HOLLER HAS A CREATURE

An Introduction to Holler Life   73
The Bone Lady (Amqui, Quebec)   75
The Devil Spider (Hudson Valley, New York)   77
The Jersey Devil (Pine Barrens, New Jersey)   78
The Bogey Men (Olympia, Kentucky)   80
The Pope Lick Monster (Louisville, Kentucky)   82
The Rat Man (Jackson, Kentucky)   86
The White Thangs (Various, Alabama and West Virginia)   87
The Snallygaster (South Mountain, Maryland)   88
The Snarly Yow (Harpers Ferry, West Virginia)   90
The Wampus Cat (Appalachian Mountain Legend, Various States)   91
The Lizard Man of Scape Ore Swamp
    (Bishopville, South Carolina)   92
Bunny Man Bridge (Clifton, Virginia)   94
Ol' Pete (Rutledge, Tennessee)   97
The Man at the Crossroads (Harlan, Kentucky)   98
It Bites (Evington, Virginia)   99

PART V. THE SASQUATCH ENCOUNTERS

Bigfoot in the Appalachians   103
The Ohio Grassman (Eastern Ohio)   105
The Minerva Monster (Minerva, Ohio)   107
The Apple Devils (Marlinton, West Virginia)   108
Orange Eyes (Mill Lake, Ohio)   110
The White Thang (Blakeslee, Pennsylvania)   111

PART VI. EERIE LOCATIONS

Mammoth Cave (Cave City, Kentucky)   113
The Mushroom Mines (Lawton, Kentucky)   117
Wright-Patterson Air Force Base (Dayton, Ohio)   120

Conclusion   127
Appendix I. The Crestview Incident: Indrid Cold in Florida   131
Appendix II. The Bench Leg of Goeble Ridge
    (Louisa, Kentucky)   135
About the Author and Illustrator   141

ACKNOWLEDGEMENTS

The creation of any book is usually not just down to the author and the illustrator. We would be remiss in not thanking those who have helped create the book you now hold in your hands or on your e-reader device. We would like to thank the following people in no particular order.

Jeff Wamsley from the Mothman Museum in Point Pleasant, for having an incredible collection to look through. Dave Spinks from Dave Spinks' World of Weird, for his assistance and guidance to local stories. Andrew Smith from the Flatwoods Monster Museum, for such a keen insight into Braxxie. Kyle Kadel of the International Paranormal Museum and Research Center, for his kindness and generosity. Frank Feschnio, for his amazing research on the Flatwoods Monster. Shannon LeGro of Into the Fray Radio, for all her support. Seth Breedlove from Small Town Monsters, for inspiration and support. Ben Armstrong of Netherworld, for running the best haunted attraction in the world. Nancy Alloy from Books at Park Place, for helping us get all the research books no matter how obscure. Chris and Monique Muncy, for allowing us the use of your wonderful home in the mountains of Kentucky for our base camp. Laura Kelleher, for continued love and support. Kathy Schultz and Paul Schultz, for helping to keep the van on the road. Dan Blastorah, for all his support as well.

We would also like to thank Elizabeth and Callie Muncy. We could not ask for better kids to put up with all our crazy. Some call it chaos—we call it family.

Finally, we have to thank the amazing team at Arcadia Publishing for being so generous with us. Joe Gartrell is a super editor and put up with all the fun global pandemic delays. Thanks to Ryan Finn and his master editing, without whom we would have forgotten a whole monster. To Crystal Murray, thanks for all you do to keep our books in print. Jonny Foster and Katie Perry are our incredible team of publicists that help keep us on the road at events and speaking engagements.

Lastly, we would like to thank *you* for buying and enjoying our first book outside of Florida. We hope you enjoy the show!

INTRODUCTION

Greetings, traveler. So, you picked up this book and are thinking, "Isn't this the *Eerie Florida* guy?" Yes! I am that guy.

I have spent three decades collecting and researching the myths, monsters and legends from the dark side of the Sunshine State. If you would like to investigate those, you can pick up our best sellers *Eerie Florida*, *Freaky Florida* and *Creepy Florida*, all of which are available from The History Press. We would love you if you got them all.

Now you are probably wondering, "How does this Floridian think he has the gall to write about the Appalachians? Does he know anything about the monsters and legends up here? He has probably seen *The Mothman Prophecies* and maybe even *The Legend of Boggy Creek*, but can he know anything about this area? He is used to conquistadors, pirate ghosts, skunk apes and Robert the Doll. What does he know about the local lore, legends and monsters of this area?"

In truth, I am a child of the Appalachians. I lived most of my early life in and around the Ohio and Kanawha Valleys. I spent every weekend in the woods along the Kentucky and West Virginia border. We went fishing and hunting near the Big Sandy River and what is now the Yatesville Lake State Park. I grew up on local folklore and ghost stories. Is it any wonder that I simply transferred that obsession to Florida when I moved there?

So, why come back to it now? Was I bored with Florida after three books? Not at all. We were investigating a story for a future Florida book when a name came up that it led us back to the land I once called home. It was from there that we started to snowball into other cases and legends that were loosely tied into a timeline of events that spanned large portions of the Appalachian Mountains and lots right in the very heart of them.

Before we get into the meat of things, here's a little history for you on the mountain range itself. We won't delve too much into the prehistoric, but I think a general overview of the area we are going to cover and how it got its name is in order.

In 1528, one of our old Florida-based Spanish conquistadors named Pánfilo de Narváez sent an expedition to the northern coast of what was then La Florida. Near what is now Tallahassee, they discovered a Native American settlement. They noted the name of this village as Apalachen. The Spanish began to refer to the village as Apalachee and used that name for the tribe. Shortly after, Pánfilo marched north into what would then be called the Appalachian Territory.

A decade or so later, another conquistador named Hernando de Soto sent cartographers into the area from Florida. This would be around the year 1540. The mapmakers chose to apply the name "Appalachian" to the mountains and not just the territory at this point. It was still alternated as Appalachian and Apalachen as late as the 1600s on Spanish maps.

Sometime later, French, and Canadian explorers were mapping what would be the northern portion of this range. The Lenape tribe of Native Americans took them to a range marked by the Allegheny River. The word is supposed to mean "fine river," but no one is totally certain of the translation. That river only flows through a small portion of the mountains in what is now Pennsylvania and portions of West Virginia. Noted naturalist John Muir used the term "Alleghanies" to describe the southern Appalachians.

It would not be until late into the nineteenth century that the name of the mountains would be generally agreed on. The Alleghenies are generally considered the part of the range that follows from the Allegheny Front and the Susquehanna River to the north and east. And they head about four hundred miles south to the New River valley in West Virginia.

Modern maps show that the Appalachians run north as far as Newfoundland in Canada and run south through New River in West Virginia and contain parts of the Blue Ridge Mountains in Kentucky as well. They run more than 1,500 miles into Central Alabama. The Smoky Mountains are a noted subrange through Tennessee and North Carolina. Geologically speaking, the Ouachita Mountains that go through Arkansas and Oklahoma were once a part of this range as well but became separated through geologic activity in ancient history.

Now, this is a huge area and marks the divide between the eastern United States and the Midwest. Washington Irving once even suggested renaming the United States to Appalachia since it represented so much of the country at that time in the early 1800s. Today, it is more of a loosely defined area of the central-eastern United States. Even that definition of boundaries has been fought over for generations.

In 1960, the Council of Appalachian Governors, which included ten states, united to seek federal help for the mountainous portions of their states. These areas lagged far behind the rest of the United States in terms of income, education, healthcare and transportation. In 1963, President John F. Kennedy formed the Appalachian Regional Commission to help bring federal money to the areas that were hardest hit. To this day, the area is a focal point for government attempts to rebuild infrastructure, leveraging the cultural and natural assets and creating economic opportunities.

When you ask many about Appalachia, many still think of the rivalry between moonshiners and law enforcement dating back to President Rutherford B. Hayes trying to push the need for the Whiskey Tax in the late 1870s. This stigma stayed until way past the Prohibition period of the 1920s. Clan feuding and continuation of Civil War–era disputes marred some areas—the most famous of these being of the Hatfield and McCoy feud. Journalists of the time may have sensationalized the stereotypes. In reality, many of these feuds were simple political players vying for power.

To understand this book, you must realize that we needed to cut through all the yellow journalism of the area. We had to dig past sensational headlines about "Mothman" and the "Flatwoods Monster." We had to investigate more than just unclassified Project Blue Book documents and stories of coal mine ghosts. I was from here and needed to get to the heart of some of these legends. Boots on the ground would be needed. This book would take a lot longer than some day trips to the other coast of Florida.

With this vast area and so many stories to choose from, explaining this project to my publisher took some doing. As we chased leads and interviewed witnesses, a strange pattern emerged over a concentrated area. We realized that we could focus on a select portion and on a specific timeline of events that seemed to be at the very heart of it all. Once we settled on this, a clear picture began to form that blew away all our preconceptions of every one of these cases.

What does all that boil down to you, dear reader? You are going to join us on a journey through folklore and history, all the way to recent interviews and eyewitness statements. We have gone on UFO watches, ghost investigations,

Sasquatch hunts and numerous dives into every archive that would allow us through several states. I have interviewed many firsthand experiencers, experts and fellow investigators. We made many trips to locations from our base camp at my family land in Eastern Kentucky.

In one section of the book, there is a collection of what we refer to as "holler monsters." These are stories that are difficult to pin down with historical facts. Most are folk tales and legends that have been told for generations but never seem to leave the valley or family circles that originated them. I am happy to present some of these in these pages for the first time in print.

Of course, in 2020, the world suffered from the global pandemic of COVID-19. Trips were delayed, some interviews were canceled and many contacts sadly were lost. Thankfully, the extra time gave us even more stories. Thanks to virtual meetings becoming the "new normal," we were eventually able to speak with even more witnesses and folklore experts who would normally have been impossible to meet.

Mark and Kari Schultz in front of one the Braxton County monster chairs in Flatwoods. *Photo by the author.*

My wonderful wife, Kari Schultz, whose illustrations and photography abound throughout this work, was of course at my side for all of this. She was excited at the prospect of so many new monsters and legends to explore. We hope you enjoy the dividends of her labor.

Finally, my dear reader, I feel it is only right to give you a friendly word of warning before we begin. What you will find in the coming pages may shock you. It may thrill you. It might even horrify you. So, if you feel you do not have the disposition to carry on…well, don't say we didn't warn you.

MARK MUNCY,
December 23, 2021

PART I

THE APPALACHIAN TRIANGLE, 1950s AND 1960s

INDRID COLD

Parkersburg, West Virginia

On a cold, early November night in 1966 on Interstate 77 just before the Route 47 interchange, a salesman named Woodrow "Woody" Derenberger had a close encounter that is still talked about to this day in hushed tones. The next day was when the world learned of Indrid Cold, also known as the "Smiling Man."

A few weeks earlier in the foothills of the Appalachians in New Jersey, two young boys were walking home when they encountered a strange man in a green suit. The boys, Martin Munov and James Yanchitis, saw the tall man staring at them from behind a fence. When they steered clear, the man kept smiling at them and began to follow at a clip.

The boys began to run and got home safely. They told their folks about the incident, and it made a stir among locals. Notably, though, the boys' story had odd details. They claimed that the man had strange features, like no nose and no ears. They made frequent mention of his unusual smile. The police and press mostly laughed it off. The whole affair was quickly forgotten.

Then came that night on November 2 a few hundred miles away on a highway along the Ohio and West Virginia border. Woody Derenberger was driving home and saw a car speed past him. It appeared that the car was being chased by a large flying cylindrical object. Woody could not believe his eyes. He described the flying craft as looking like a cylindrical chimney.

The craft pulled in front of him and began to slow down—not suddenly but slowly, so Woody slowed down with it. Eventually, he parked on the side of the interstate next to the hovering craft. A door opened from the cylinder, and out stepped a tall man in a shining and sparkling green suit.

The figure went to the right side of Woody's truck and asked him to open the window on that side. Woody did and noticed the man's unusual smile. He had to ask himself if the strange man had actually spoken or had he simply heard him ask to roll down the window.

Woody kept talking to the strange man for a long period. The man told him his name was Indrid Cold. Indrid told Woody that he meant him no harm. He was a visitor from the planet Lanulos in the Ganymede Galaxy.

Indrid wanted to know all he could about Earth and its inhabitants. Indrid spoke telepathically, but Woody answered by speaking. Indrid asked questions about the city nearby, which was Parkersburg, West Virginia. When Woody told him that most people only worked and shopped there but lived nearby, Indrid told him that they called those locations on his planet "gatherings."

The conversation went on for some time. Other cars passed, and Woody wondered if anyone else was seeing the strange man and his "kerosene chimney"-shaped craft hovering beside the road. After some time, Cold simply stopped asking questions and went back to the craft. Woody saw another arm reach out from the door to help him into his hovering vehicle. Woody watched as this strange craft flew away quickly into the sky. Before leaving Indrid told him, "Mr. Derenberger, we will be seeing you again."

Not sure what to do or who to tell all this to, Woody told his wife. He told her that Cold had asked him to speak to journalists. She convinced him to call the police. A short while later, they came to interview him, as did the local radio station. Glenn Wilson recorded a thirty-minute interview with Woody about the incident. The recording of it is available online. The original tapes are on display at the Mothman Museum in Point Pleasant, not too far from Parkersburg.

If you listen to the whole interview, it is amazing the amount of detail in Woody's retelling of the encounter. Listening to it, you cannot help but tell that he was shaken up by the experience. The reporters aired the interview, but it was not picked up much further than the local channels at the time.

A few weeks later, there was a reported sighting of Indrid Cold as his "Grinning Man" persona in the town of Point Pleasant, West Virginia. This encounter was when the Lily family had been plagued by poltergeist-like activity in their home. Their daughter, Linda, woke up one night and

The original reel-to-reel recordings of the interview with Woodrow "Woody" Derenberger about his encounter with Indrid Cold are on display at the Mothman Museum in Point Pleasant, West Virginia. *Photo by the author.*

described a figure very similar to Indrid Cold's description from Woody Derenberger's account. The figure was standing in her room and then simply vanished.

Most investigators discount this as a true sighting, but John Keel used it to tie Indrid Cold to the Mothman stories he had been investigating due to the similarities and the fascinating story of Derenberger's encounter with Indrid Cold. This would be quite influential in bringing Indrid Cold to wider knowledge thanks to the movie *The Mothman Prophecies* and its infamous Chapstick scene.

Woody Derenberger would later author a book about return visits from Indrid and other aliens from Lanulos. His book *Visitors from Lanulos* goes into details about Indrid and the alien's own family, who apparently were living among the humans here on Earth. The book also describes how Indrid Cold took Woody to his home planet on a few occasions. The Derenberger family claimed that Woody would disappear often for weeks or even months at a time during these visits.

According to Woody's daughter, Taunia Derenberger, in her book *Beyond Lanulos*, Indrid and his crew are still around to this very day. They have barely aged in the fifty-plus years since that fateful night. They come to visit her and keep an eye on the entire Derenberger family tree.

Indrid Cold would later be tied to the Men in Black phenomenon. These mysterious men appeared shortly after the Mothman sightings rose to prominence in Point Pleasant in 1962. The men wore strange black suits and had unusual mannerisms. Most notably, when speaking, they seemed to put the wrong emphasis on syllables in words as though they were foreign agents.

After people witnessed UFOs and related phenomena, those involved would be approached by these unusual Men in Black. Many would say that the men asked them to keep quiet about the event. Some even claimed that they were threatened with incarceration by the government or even physical harm. There are very few records of their encounters but lots of anecdotes from those who encountered them.

Indrid is connected to them, as several encounters were eerily similar to his unusual description. However, there may be a more concrete link between them from the Crestview UFO sighting event from Miami in April 1967. Dozens of students and teachers at a school just north of Miami saw several unusual craft outside their school. Most of the witnesses were questioned by the military and some black-suited investigators. The father of one of the young children scribbled down the names of those who questioned his boy. The military men had normal names. The strange "government man" with them was named Cold.

Indrid Cold, as described by Woody and Taunia Derenberger. *Illustration by Kari Schultz.*

Although it has been more than fifty years since the questioning, the witness remembered both the sighting and the questioning vividly. The newspapers claimed the next day that the UFOs were merely helicopters on maneuvers from the nearby navy base. The sighting details are in the appendix of this book.

The young witness remembered the military men asking all the questions during his interview, but the "government man" was only staring at him with a strange smile. He said the memory gives him chills to this very day. If true, this could mean that Indrid began working for the government to help investigate other UFO events.

Talking to Taunia Derenberger, she claimed that Indrid is not only still alive, but also that he and his family visit her frequently. She reported his death in 2019 but then recanted. She has continued to document their conversations as her father did before her. Another book from her is forthcoming at the time of this writing in late 2021.

THE MOTHMAN

Point Pleasant, West Virginia

It is impossible to discuss the strange and unusual history of the Appalachians without being drawn deep into the circle of the mysterious Mothman of Point Pleasant, West Virginia. His shadow is so great that he has permeated pop culture; even a blockbuster movie was made of his story. We will try to separate fact from fiction here.

The first sighting of the creature that would become known as Mothman came on the night of November 12, 1966. Five gravediggers were working in a cemetery on a hill in Clendenin, West Virginia. One of them saw "a brown human being" jumping into the air from some nearby trees. The thing flew over them. The men were aghast, as it was not a bird but more like a man with wings. There would be other sightings soon to follow.

A few days later on the night of November 15, two married couples were driving just past Point Pleasant in an area near an old, abandoned World War II munitions plant. The area was referred to as the "TNT area." It was a well-known place to go and hide from the prying eyes of the town and let off some steam.

While they were driving, one of the young ladies spotted two large eyes that glowed back at them. As she alerted the others, they described seeing the creature as "shaped like a man, but bigger. Maybe, six or seven feet tall. It had big wings folded against its back." It had one wing tangled in a fence. It used muscular hands to pull itself free and then ran off into the nearby factory.

The driver finally broke in terror and gunned the engine of the car, driving away as fast as he could. A minute passed and suddenly the creature was on the hillside near the road next to them. Its wings were spread wide, and it rose into the air like a rocket. It kept pace with their car, which was doing well over one hundred miles per hour. "That bird kept right up with us," was the statement from one of the witnesses. They drove quickly back to town. It appeared perched at several locations along the road as they sped back to town as though it was moving at incredible speeds or even teleporting instantaneously. The creature stopped following them as they neared the city limits of Point Pleasant.

The group in the car felt so uneasy that they drove straight to the Sheriff's Office. Deputy Sheriff Millard Halstead had the witnesses lead him out to the site of the encounter.

Often forgotten is that they were not the only ones to see the creature that night. Another group of four claimed to see a giant "bird" at several different times that same evening in a nearby area. About ninety miles away in the town of Salem, West Virginia, Newell Partridge, a local contractor, said that his television suddenly went dark at around 10:30 p.m. He then said it turned back on with a strange pattern on the screen, and he heard a loud, high-pitched whine coming

The Mothman statue in Point Pleasant is iconic, but it is an artistic representation, not similar to sighting descriptions. *Photo by the author.*

from outside. "It sounded like a generator winding up," he was quoted as saying. His dog, Bandit, began howling outside. Partridge went outside to have a look.

Once outside, he could see that Bandit was facing the barn. He turned on a flashlight to see what his dog was so intently observing. Two red circles that looked like eyes and glowed like bike reflectors greeted the beam of his flashlight. Bandit ran off toward the eyes, and Partridge went inside to get his gun.

Partridge was too shaken up to go back out. The next morning, he realized that Bandit had not returned. A few days passed, and he saw the articles about the incident in Point Pleasant. That was when he realized he had seen the same thing. Bandit was never seen again.

In one of the original accounts, one of the witnesses said that when they fled back into town, they passed the body of a large dog on the side of the road. When they returned later, it was gone. They had even stopped to look for it with the deputy sheriff, as it had been there just minutes before. Some researchers feel that might have been Bandit.

The next day, on November 16, Deputy Halstead and some of the witnesses held a press conference. The deputy assured the press that he had known all the witnesses and that they should be taken very seriously. Many of the local press knew the witnesses as well and vouched for them.

One of the local papers decided to call the creature Mothman due to the popularity of the 1966 Batman TV series starring Adam West. Even though the descriptions of the creature were nothing like a moth, the name stuck and has been associated with the creature ever since.

Hunters and curious onlookers swarmed the area of Point Pleasant in the aftermath of this press conference. The old munitions factory was now Mothman ground zero. The TNT area around it was the perfect place for a monster's lair. There are acres and acres of wooded land. The concrete domes used to store explosives when the plant was active dotted the forest. There were even tunnels to explore to look for the creature.

The area is now the McClintock Wildlife Preserve and is a haven for hikers and nature enthusiasts. Is it any wonder that people thought the Mothman could have hidden out here for months if not for years to come?

The night after the press conference, Mrs. Marcella Bennett observed a strange red light in the sky over the old factory. She could not figure out what it was but knew it was not a helicopter or a plane. She drove to the nearby Thomas family farmhouse to see if they could figure it out. Once there, she was shocked by a close encounter with the creature. "It rose up slowly from the ground. A big gray thing. Bigger than a man with terrible glowing eyes," she later said in an interview.

She grabbed her baby, whom she had brought with her, and ran into the house. The Thomas family were panicked and locked up the house once Mrs. Bennet and her baby were safely inside. According to the family, the creature shuffled onto the porch and looked in the windows at them. The police were called, but the monster had vanished before they arrived.

The incident so shook up Mrs. Bennett that she sought aid for her mental health. She claimed that the monster was haunting her dreams so badly that sleep was elusive. She later claimed that the monster might have visited her home as well.

For nearly a year, strange stories and encounters were seemingly a daily occurrence in the area. UFO enthusiasts swarmed the town. Sightings of the infamous Men in Black began to be reported. Among the researchers coming to town, there was no one more famous than John Keel.

Right and opposite: The varied descriptions of the Mothman. He's most often described in more recent sightings as a "flying sasquatch" with a sunken head. This matches some of the original observations before they were influenced by artistic representations. *Illustrations by Kari Schultz.*

Keel believed that the Mothman was not extraterrestrial. He felt that it was a supernatural being. He had written extensively on man's encounters with the paranormal for years. He was somewhat controversial in his writings, as he dismissed the idea of aliens and felt that these strange encounters were with angels, demons, ghosts and "the gods of old."

As the primary record keeper of the Mothman case, he wrote that he interviewed more than one hundred people who had witnessed the creature in the year following the initial sighting. Every report stated that the creature was somewhere around six or seven feet tall. It was broad and wide and shuffled as it walked. The creature's eyes were somewhere near the top of the shoulders. Its skin was either a dusky gray or a dark brown. It had long wings that allowed it to glide; most never saw them flap. The wings were batlike, but some said they were covered with fur; still others said feathers. Most agreed that the wings were even darker colored than the rest of the creature and difficult to make out.

In action, the Mothman was able to leap into the air. "Like a helicopter," one witness famously described. It seemed to give off a strange hum as it would glide on those long wings at incredible speeds.

Keel's witness reports state that the creature never spoke. The only sounds it seemed capable of were a strange high-pitched squeaking or squeal. Mrs.

Bennett claimed that it would keen like a woman screaming.

Keel famously documented his time in Point Pleasant after he arrived in December 1966, right at the height of Mothman fever. He noted strange activity with the televisions and phones of the area. He documented a large number of poltergeist-like encounters at many of the homes in the immediate area. The sheer volume of it all convinced Keel that all of the reports of these strange encounters he was collecting were most definitely connected.

One of the most famous related incidents was when Mary Hyre, a reporter for the Athens, Ohio newspaper the *Messenger*, had her own odd encounter. She was the Point Pleasant correspondent and one of the main reporters chronicling the Mothman and UFO sightings in the area. She noted in one article that she had taken hundreds of calls one evening from the area after some strange lights were seen in the skies over the TNT area.

In January 1967, a man walked into her office at the paper. She noted that he had strange eyes behind very thick glasses. He was noticeably short and had black hair in a bowl cut. Something about this man unnerved her greatly. The man spoke in a strange, pausing voice and eventually asked for directions to the town of Welsh, West Virginia. She assumed the man must have had some sort of speech impediment. "He kept getting closer and closer to me and his funny eyes were staring at me almost hypnotically," Hyre said later of the encounter.

At this point, Hyre called for help, and the newspaper's circulation manager came in. They continued to speak to the unusual man. According to Hyre, her phone rang, and when she answered it, the man picked up a pen from her desk. He looked at it like he had never seen one before. Then he ran away laughing like a mad man.

Hyre saw the man one more time several weeks later. When he realized that she had seen him, he ran off in a panic. Suddenly, a large black car came around the corner, and the little man jumped into it as it sped away. This led to tie the Men in Black further to the Mothman phenomenon since Hyre was one of the main reporters of the sightings of the creature.

Mothman fever had died down by the following November. There were still reports of strange activity, but the holidays seemed to push it out from the headlines of the papers. Life was moving on in Point Pleasant.

On December 15, 1967, the Silver Bridge, a seven-hundred-foot bridge that crossed from Point Pleasant into Ohio, suddenly collapsed with five o'clock traffic. Dozens of vehicles with trapped people fell into the wintery waters of the Ohio River. Forty-six people tragically lost their lives that night. Forty-four of them are buried at the Gallipolis, Ohio cemetery, just across the water from Point Pleasant. Two of the victims were never found.

The Silver Bridge disaster was the new major headline across America. The horror of this unforeseen tragedy is still felt to this day in the town. Keel and other researchers claim that the Mothman might have been some sort of warning of the impending disaster.

To many, the Mothman sightings disappear after this tragic event. The newspapers certainly did not want to carry headlines of the strange creature after such a tragic event. There were still reported sightings to Mary Hyre and others, but the papers simply did not make room for them.

During the weeks after the disaster, Hyre once again met with another strange man in her office. This one came in with a black suit and black tie and looked like he was of East Asian descent. She said this man also spoke haltingly and with an unplaceable accent. He was the first person in weeks to ask about things other than the bridge disaster. He wanted to know about local UFO sightings. She said she was too busy to speak with him but offered her file of related news articles. He said that he wanted the reports of sightings that were not in the papers. He insisted on speaking with her. She had him removed from her office.

She received word the next day that the same man visited many of the witnesses of recent encounters at their homes. Many had not been reported on. Every person told Hyre that he had made them feel afraid and out of sorts. He told them that he was a reporter from Cambridge, Ohio. In a slip, he told one of the families he did not know where Columbus, Ohio was, even though Cambridge is almost a suburb of Columbus.

Keel ended his book *The Mothman Prophecies* with the Silver Bridge disaster. The newspapers in the area had already stopped publishing sightings. Some debunkers had claimed that the creature was merely a sandhill crane or a large barn owl that many had misidentified. Most of the witnesses were certain that it was no large bird. Still with interest waning, it appeared that the Mothman had disappeared—at least to those who only followed news reports of the creature.

In recent years, the Mothman has returned in popularity. This has allowed post-1967 sightings to come to light again. The creature never left and was still sighted often throughout the years. Though not as frequently reported as in the past, Mothman encounters are still documented to this day in areas all over eastern Ohio and throughout West Virginia. There are many credible sources that definitively say that it is no bird or hoax.

One recent encounter from 2018 was when a postal truck driver was crossing the New River Bridge, the third-highest suspension bridge in the world and only a short drive from Point Pleasant. He saw an unusually large creature with a reddish glow to its eyes following him on the bridge as night was falling. He realized that it was doing nearly seventy miles an hour and flew along beside him over the huge gap below. He described it as a flying Sasquatch with a ten-foot wingspan. He claimed that he had never thought of the Mothman as his encounter. He thought it was a drone or some strange flying Bigfoot hoax until it turned toward him and stared at him with its glowing red eyes. It flew away from him, diving out of sight shortly after that moment, and he quickly reported the sighting to the police.

Outside of the Mothman Museum in downtown Point Pleasant, right next to the statue. *Photo by the author.*

One of the "TNT domes" in McClintok Wildlife District near Point Pleasant. Be careful when exploring these, as some are still considered to be unsafe. *Photo by the author.*

The Mothman phenomenon has expanded all over the world with sightings of "flying humanoids" being reported in such diverse places as Chicago and India. These sightings are usually more gargoyle-like, but the press still refer to them as Mothman.

Many assume the sighting of the creature to be an omen of disaster, thanks to the connections to the original sightings and the Silver Bridge disaster one year later. Keel himself seemed inclined to believe that theory. Others claim that Chief Cornstalk laid a curse on the town after he was murdered, but that was debunked when it was found to be from a theatrical play.

Whatever Mothman was or is, we may never know for certain. People have certainly encountered something. Many were so shaken to their core by their encounters that they have never been the same since.

The town of Point Pleasant has embraced the Mothman now. The small town hosts a Mothman Festival in September that draws in thousands of cryptozoological and paranormal fans from all over the world. The highlight of the trip includes visiting the Mothman Museum, which houses an amazing collection of all things Mothman, Men in Black and more. The museum was created and owned by Jeff Wamsley. He even created the festival, which has grown exponentially every year.

The famous Mothman statue is right outside the museum. An artist and retired welder named Bob Roach was commissioned to make it by the town after the movie *The Mothman Prophecies* became a hit. John Keel returned to Point Pleasant for the unveiling in 2003. The steel statue's creature is ripped and muscular, with gypsy moth–like wings. The statue worked like a beacon and has turned the town into a fun tourist destination.

Although the old munitions plant has been torn down, the concrete domes still litter the McClintock Wildlife District nearby. Mothman enthusiasts often drive the short distance from the heart of Point Pleasant to go looking for their own Mothman encounter in the TNT area, just like the young couples who started it all so many years ago.

THE GRAFTON MONSTER

Grafton, West Virginia

The town of Grafton in north-central West Virginia has a lot of historical significance. Most famously, it is the town that invented Mother's Day. Grafton was a boomtown in the early days of coal mining and the railroad. It is also the home of both of West Virginia's National Cemeteries. All of that seems to fall by the wayside due to a strange encounter on a fateful night.

The Baltimore and Ohio Railroads met in Grafton, which helped the businesses of the town and built its rapid expansion in the late 1800s. As the business grew, it made living there difficult due to smoke from the railroads and factories. The economic situation in the town began to deteriorate quickly in the late 1940s. The Carr China Plant and the Hazel Atlas Glass Plant closed in the late 1950s, which left much of the town without work.

Grafton began to rally in the early 1960s. There were numerous attempts to return industry to the town. The railroads had been rerouted, and it was not far from the interstate. It even won the National Civic League's All-America City award in 1962. The town was recovering.

On the evening of June 16, 1964, reporter Robert Cockrell was driving home from a late night at the paper. He made this trip every day. As he passed one turn and began to head down a particularly dark stretch of road that went through the woods near his home, he noticed what he thought was a large boulder blocking the right side of the road.

As he knew of no rockslides in the area and drove this road quite frequently, he was curious about where the boulder could have come from. Then he realized that it was moving—the boulder was alive. It had to be some hulking beast that stood at least eight feet tall. The beast had a large width and seemed very muscular. The head of the creature was either sunken in or small. It was covered in a slick skin like that of a seal. He later felt it might have had very pale wet skin.

As the giant beast shambled farther out of the way, Cockrell seized his chance. He sped past the large creature and quickly made his way home without ever looking back. Cockrell was unable to come to grips with what he had just seen. He sat down and began to type up an account of the strange experience for the *Grafton Sentinel*. He then decided to call some friends to see if they could go out and find the monster he had just encountered.

The group of friends went out to the spot and found only signs of crushed grass. They heard a strange whistling noise that seemed to haunt them. After a few hours of searching, they gave up the hunt, and Cockrell decided that he would not publish his encounter.

A few days later, he changed his mind. He honestly thought that, at best, no one would even bother to read the story. He secretly held hopes that someone else had seen the strange creature and that his report might bring forth more witnesses. He did not expect the frenzy that was about to ensue.

The town was flooded with hunters and gangs of armed men hoping to capture the creature. Many of these groups were heavily armed and charged into the nearby woods. After a few close calls involving shots being fired, the sheriff insisted on a retraction. A follow-up article on June 19 came out in the *Grafton Sentinel*. The article reads as follows.

> *Grafton's alleged "monster," reportedly the personification of the active imaginations of a number of teenagers, couldn't have shown up in the Riverside drive area if it wanted to on Thursday night, too many teenagers and adults were roaming that section of the city. At approximately 10 p.m., it was reported that cars were almost bumper-to-bumper along the river drive and a large number of cars were pulled off the road to permit joining in the area's most popular event in recent years, "monster hunting."*
>
> *Some 20 reports from persons allegedly seeing the "monster" have been quoted since Tuesday night when the "all white creature without a discernible head," was reported seen near the city rock quarry. Wednesday night about 30 teenagers engaged in a "monster hunt," but by Thursday night the number of teenagers had doubled, and a number of adults joined in the action.*

After the running of this article, the police began to chase away the crowds. It may have slowed some of the hunters and the frenzy around the Grafton

The Grafton Monster is either headless or has a sunken-in head. It almost appears as a moving rock or has skin slick like a seal, depending on the account. *Illustration by Kari Schultz.*

Monster encounter for a short while. Cockrell, however, was pleased to see that he was getting some corroboration as other witnesses came forward.

Most encounters described the creature as being eight to ten feet tall. Everyone described how it was white or gray in color. Everyone described how thick and muscular the creature seemed to be—how methodical it moved. Nearly every sighting described the sunken or nonexistent head. Several reports claimed to have seen the creature many times over the years.

As with the Mothman and many other strange creatures, many folks claimed to see strange lights in the sky or other UFO-type phenomena around the time of their encounter with the Grafton Monster. Cockrell reached out to UFO researcher Gray Barker. They interviewed many witnesses together, and Barker formed a report.

One encounter from the report described an account where a man encountered the creature early in the morning. Startled, the man turned and ran to his truck. He turned and looked back and saw that the creature had run into the trees. "I heard a whooshing sound and a bright light appeared above the tree line." He added that he did not go back for his fishing gear for two days.

The police announced that their investigation had come to the conclusion that the Grafton Monster was merely a hoax. Cockrell had simply misidentified a man pushing a wheelbarrow filled with boxes. The other sightings had been "Spring Fever" pranks and simple overactive imagination. The frenzy died down quickly.

Barker, however, was convinced that the monster was linked with UFO activity in the area. He wrote a lengthy article that somehow never saw print. It is located in the Gray Barker Collection in the Clarksburg-Harrison Public Library in West Virginia. What is interesting is that Barker was infamous as the man who coined the concept of Men in Black. He often was known to have created a few fictional documents that wound up putting him at odds with other UFO experts. If he was creating another fictional stir with the Grafton Monster, why did he never publish this story?

Cockrell, in his later years, recanted his account of the encounter despite claiming that it was authentic through most of his days. Between this and Barker's involvement, it leads many into thinking that the whole Grafton Monster was nothing more than a hoax. However, there are still several families in the area who talk of sightings of the creature that predate Cockrell's initial article.

THE HOPKINSVILLE GOBLINS

Kelly, Kentucky

In Christian County, Kentucky, in August 1955, a strange encounter would change the history of the area forever.

Geraldine Sutton-Stith, daughter of Elmer "Lucky" Sutton, has spoken about that fateful night often and has also authored several books on the subject, including *Alien Legacy* and *The Kelly Green Men*. She is the definitive expert on the subject, as she was a firsthand witness.

The towns of Kelly and Hopkinsville, Kentucky, are remarkably similar today to what they were like in 1955. Small rural communities each with a single grocery store and small downtown area. The Sutton farm was situated just outside both in unincorporated Christian County, a good distance from both town centers.

The Sutton brothers, Elmer and John, and their family were hosting the visiting Baker family with their children. Late on that hot evening, Billy Ray Baker went out to draw water from the well. He saw a brilliant meteor shower. Elmer came out to see what was taking so long with the water. He saw the shower as well. Then, as one meteor grew larger and larger, they realized that it was a disc-shaped craft with a rainbow-like tail. It slowed as it passed over the farm and went over the nearby hill.

Not knowing what to make of their strange sighting, the two men watched for more meteors or "flying saucers." They heard what they thought was a landing, perhaps from the large craft from earlier. They packed the children quickly off to bed to be safe.

A short while later, while watching for more unusual activity, the men witnessed a strange sight. A small, peculiar, floating being came out of the woods and toward the house. This silver creature with long arms floated toward them. The little creature had no feet of note. Its arms were raised in the air over its head. Two giant yellow eyes shone from its large round head. The two men ran inside and warned their families of the strange visitor.

No one believed them until Lucky's mother, Glennie, saw the creature at the door. The men grabbed their guns and started shooting. According to their accounts, bullets bounced off the "little man." Shortly afterward, more and more of the creatures arrived, flying and floating about the farmhouse. There was a long period of gunfire from the men of the family lasting for several hours.

Finally, the men realized that they were doing no damage to the protective suits of these "aliens from Mars." They gathered their families and made a break for town. They drove to the Hopkinsville police station with their strange story.

The police organized a small force of four city police and five state troopers and went out to the farmhouse. A brief time later, they were joined by military men. The military were reported initially as air force but were later clarified to be military police officers from Fort Campbell, a nearby army base. The search of the property yielded nothing but shotgun casings and bullet holes—no signs of the goblins or their craft.

Of the eleven people in the house at the start of the evening, most packed up and fled back to their homes. The press descended on the small town the next day. The towns of Kelly and Hopkinsville tripled in population from reporters alone.

Early attempts to rationalize the encounter pointed out that most of the adult witnesses had been intoxicated. The description of the goblins seemingly matched those of the Great Horned Owls that nested in the area. That combined with the excitement of a meteor shower and it was easy to see how the men just got carried away.

The newspapers that printed the story initially called them "Tub Men," as one of the Suttons had said their ship must have carried them down like a tub. One newspaper account named them "little green men." Even though none of the witnesses ever mentioned the color green, it was too late. The press picked up the term and ran it everywhere. The Kelly Little Green Men, also known as the Hopkinsville Goblins, were here to stay.

The *Kentucky New Era* newspaper stayed in the town waiting for them to come back. The newspaper's photos are the ones most commonly associated with the incident. Public sentiment turned on the families, and the whole incident quickly became a source of ridicule for them. It would be years before they would speak of it again. The Sutton family moved away a short while after the incident.

HOW TO FIGHT SPACEMEN—'Lucky' Sutton, 26, of Kelly Station, looks up at roof of his home from where he says he shot down a "shiny little man" last night with his shotgun when some 15 strange little men reportedly invaded the Sutton yard. Seven other adults backed up Sutton's story but investigating police found no physical evidence of space ships or space men at the scene. (Messenger photo by Eddie Gaines)

Little 'Flying Tubmen' 'Invade' Town Of Kelly

By EDGAR ARNOLD JR.

An egg-shaped No. * washtub, "lit up like a streak of fire" and landed near Kelly Station, Christian County last night. So said eight nervous adults a ! four children when they burst into Hopkinsville Police Department.

After listening to the convincing story of the Kelly group Christian County officers and Hopkinsville city police called for State Police help and seven or eight police cars converged rapidly on the area. State Police headquarters at Madisonvill' sent four cars from this area to the scene 'at high speed and Hopkinsville and Christian County officers and at least one carload of Military Police sped to the scene.

No evidence of any space ship or any creatures from another

the most eager to talk of their experience. They were Billy Ray Taylor, 20, 'Lucky' Sutton, 26, and John Sutton, 27.

Here is the story they told to officers and reporters who converged on the Sutton home one-quarter mile east of Kelly Station, a town of approximately 150 population about eight miles north of Hopkinsville on US-41.

The three adults and their wives, plus Mrs. Glennie Langford, mother of the Sutton's, and O. T. Baker, brother of Mrs. Arlene Sutton, were in the house, along with four children, at about 7:20 p. m. Sunday when they noticed or object "all lighted up" glide into a field. At an estimated distance of one-quarter mile, it looked to be the size of a No. 2 washtub and was egg-shaped. They paid little attention to it, howev—

"Lucky" Sutton posed for the papers after his infamous encounter with what the papers called Tub Men from space. *Reprinted with permission from the* Messenger, *August 22, 1955.*

Decades later, as UFO sentiment turned and researchers started linking this encounter with other frequent sightings in the mid-1950s, the Sutton family started to regain some of their credibility. Interviews with some of the original officers also backed up that there was more going on that night than originally reported.

Although the military claimed that no evidence was procured, the police officers noted that the army men steered them away from the area of the potential landing area. Though not officially investigated, Project Blue Book listed the case and marked it as a hoax with no further comments. This was

One of the "Tub Men," later known as the Hopkinsville Goblins, as described in the accounts by the Sutton family. *Illustration by Kari Schultz.*

a common conclusion by any Blue Book case that involved a landing or any potential alien encounter.

The police chief at the time was Russel Greenwell, and throughout the years of interviews he had on the subject, he would say, "I don't know if there were little green men. I do know that every time over the years that I interviewed Glennie Sutton, that this look of terror or horrendous fear would come over her eyes every time we would discuss it. That look alone is something I cannot account for."

Geraldine Sutton-Stith likes to let everyone know that "if this could happen on one small family farm in the middle of America, then it could happen to anyone and anywhere."

Over the years since, there has been an occasional new report of a sighting. Nothing has ever been substantiated. This appears to have been a one-time event.

The town of Kelly now embraces the history of this event, now considered the grandfather of UFO close encounters. In late August, starting on the fiftieth anniversary of the incident, they began the Kelly Little Green Men Days Festival. Live music, arts and crafts and all sorts of fun activities celebrate the town's alien history. The event has occurred nearly every year since.

THE LOVELAND FROGMEN

Loveland, Ohio

In May 1955, just after three o'clock in the morning, an unnamed businessman was traveling along Riverside Drive along the Little Miami River. His headlights illuminated three strange figures standing alongside the road. The abnormal creatures were about three feet in height and had leathery skin. They were reptilian and left the road to go off under a nearby bridge.

The businessman watched them in awed silence for some time. They seemed to be speaking to one another in some sort of conversation. He noted that one of the figures was definitively some sort of leader. He got out of his car and tried to get closer to hear what they were saying and to get a better look.

A short distance from them, he stumbled and made too much noise. Most of the group ran off and jumped into the river. The leader suddenly raised what the witness described as a metallic wand. This cylindrical device suddenly sparked with power. The witness bounded back to his car and took off as fast as he could.

The story passed into legend, and various versions of it have been told ever since. In one version, he is a traveling salesman. In one version, they are lizard men. Another different version of the tale has the man captured by the creatures until he fights for the wand, and it goes off with a blast of lightning that scares the frog men back into the water. Other versions tie it into the Hopkinsville Goblin story from Kentucky.

A Loveland Frogman standing by the guardrail. *Illustration by Kari Schultz.*

Just when it had become completely an urban legend, a new sighting occurred, bringing it all back to the forefront of Loveland.

At 1:00 a.m. on Riverside Drive, Loveland police officer Ray Shockey had just turned past the Totes Boot Factory. He was driving alongside the Little Miami River when he was startled by an unidentified animal that ran past the front of his car. After he swung his spotlight onto the animal to identify it, he was stunned. He described the creature as being around four feet tall and about fifty to seventy-five pounds. It had leathery skin and large eyes. It looked so strange, and it was "crouched like a giant frog." It then stood erect and stepped over the nearby guardrail. Quickly it moved down the embankment and dove into the river.

Shockey did not want to file a report initially, but when he discussed it with his fellow officers, they told him of the old legend. He then decided that he had to write the report. It made a small splash in the local news at the time. Shockey noted that he was approached by numerous media outlets to describe the incident.

Two weeks into the new media frenzy in the town, a second police officer, Mark Matthews, saw an animal in the same area. He shot the reptilian beast and put it in the trunk of his car to show Shockey. It was a large iguana with no tail. Matthews assumed it was an escaped pet. Shockey confirmed that it was the same beast he had seen and could not identify it as an iguana due to it missing a tail.

Many point out that Shockey's simple misidentification of the large tailless iguana relates to the true nature of the Loveland Frogmen—simply a misidentified large pet reptile seen late at night combined with an old urban legend in the area.

Some researchers also point out that the officer's story only changed after government agents discussed the sighting with him. They theorize that he was told to change his story to debunk further inquiry into the unique to the area incident.

The muddied waters of this legend make dissecting it tricky. The original story has been told and retold so many times that it is difficult to find an accurate and definitive account. Matthews's account of the iguana also changed from having the body to shooting at the creature and missing. No iguana body was ever reported at the station. He claims that everything was just blown out of proportion.

In 2016, there was another sighting by two kids playing Pokémon Go in Cincinnati. That one turned out to be a hoax. A young man in a homemade frog costume jumped out at the kids playing the game.

However, there was another sighting in October 2018. This one was outside of a Loveland landmark that everyone in the area knows well. Chateau Laroche saw its initial construction in the mid-1920s by World War I veteran and Boy Scout troop leader Harry D. Andrews. Andrews was inspired by the chivalric code and was an avid medievalist. He wanted to inspire the code of chivalry in his troop. He named them the Knights of the Golden Trail.

The Boy Scout troop leader started building the castle by using land he had procured from selling one-year subscriptions to the *Cincinnati Enquirer*. He grabbed rocks from the nearby Little Miami River and began a fifty-year project of building his own castle. When the rock supply ran out, he made his own bricks with cement and milk crates.

Andrews named the castle after the military hospital in Chateau La Roche, where he was stationed in World War I. It was located in the southwest of France. "Rock Castle" was not quite finished when Andrews passed away in 1981. He willed it to his Boy Scout troop, and they completed it shortly after

Loveland Castle is quite a marvel to behold in the hills of Ohio. *Photo by the author.*

his death. The Knights of the Golden Trail have done extensive renovations over the years. Recently they added a greenhouse to the garden area.

Many of the volunteer "Knights" in the castle discuss of the numerous strange occurrences at the castle. Andrews brought back numerous artifacts from all over the world. Weapons, suits of armor and many stones from unique locations were worked into the castle. The volunteers say that some of these ghostly apparitions must be attached to these artifacts.

A ghostly figure in chainmail is seen walking up the stairs in one area, over and over. One shadowy figure frequents a room with several medieval swords on display. A few sightings of Harry Andrews himself have been reported by volunteers who knew him. Harry died when a trash fire on the grounds got out of hand and severely burned him. He succumbed to his injuries from the fire. His ghost is frequently seen at the castle.

As we were finishing up this book, an account from a visitor to the castle named Tim Macomber came to us. He was staying nearby the castle and had planned a visit to it the next day. He drove by the place after hours on the way to his hotel. Knowing of the castle's spooky reputation, he and his group were eager to visit it the next day. He was planning on joining the ghost tour offered at the castle the next evening. While nearing the castle, he saw strange lights in the sky.

Being near Cincinnati airport, he originally did not think anything unusual about the lights in the sky until he noticed that they were moving in strange patterns. The lights swirled, and the group thought it might be some sort of drone race. The lights pulsed strangely and then shot up into the sky at an impossible speed.

The group realized that the lights had been over some woods just a short distance from the castle. The group went along the road and saw large glowing yellow eyes watching them from the woods. "I panned my light at the eyes," Tim Macomber described. "I was stunned when I saw the frog-like face. Was this the Loveland Frogman? I had come to look for ghosts, not an urban legend. I was totally unprepared."

Tim and his friends scrambled for their phones and cameras, but the creature quickly dove into the water. They described it as about four feet tall and very much more like a toad than Kermit. They have frequently traveled back to the area, hoping for another encounter. They still investigated the ghosts at the castle but were eager to look for other unusual phenomena.

"I was a ghost hunter and scoffed at UFOs, Bigfoot and especially frogmen," Tim wrote. "Now I look at every avenue and realize there might be more to all of these things. I never take anything for granted now."

Loveland is a short drive from nearby Cincinnati and well worth a visit. Look at the castle as an achievement of what one man can build. Explore the haunted history of the local bridges and Chateau Laroche. Just remember to keep an eye open for large amphibious creatures that might be lurking around a dark corner in the road along the Little Miami River.

THE FLATWOODS MONSTER

Flatwoods, West Virginia

On September 12, 1952, two brothers and their friend saw a strange light in the sky over the mountains of Braxton County, West Virginia. The events that followed led to one of the most documented encounters with a possible extraterrestrial being in history. All of the surrounding information can be overwhelming for those trying to summarize the encounter.

There is no greater expert on the "Flatwoods Monster" than author and researcher Frank Feschino. Frank has spent nearly twenty years investigating this case and UFO phenomena in general. He has written two books of note on the subject of UFOs and the definitive book on the Flatwoods incident. Both have been recently updated with even more newly discovered material.

Frank says that to fully understand what happened on that fateful night in September in the Appalachian Mountains, you must first understand what was going on in 1952. That year saw an unprecedented wave of UFO sightings all over the United States. A famous encounter was seen over Washington, D.C. in White House air space. The U.S. Air Force had the newly formed Project Blue Book look into these matters.

There were a large number of fatal air tragedies during this period. Many veteran combat pilots, along with the aircraft, were lost in freak accidents or training errors. The public was generally not informed of this and reporting on most of the incidents is cursory. Researchers like Frank feel that this was to keep the public from going into mass hysteria.

Major Donald Keyhoe authored a book in 1973 call *Aliens in Space*. The retired U.S. marine major had documented many UFO sightings and wrote about a government cover-up to hide the truth about these sightings. In the book, Keyhoe claims that the enormous number of fatal air accidents was a cover-up story to hide reprisal attacks from UFOs that were being attempted to be shot down by air force jets.

There were more than six hundred freak accidents with fully experienced pilots during this period—pilots who were World War II and Korean Conflict veterans. Were they being lost in a secret war with UFOs? Keyhoe claimed that several pilots had been instructed to do anything in their power to "bring them down" when it came to UFOs. They wanted the extraterrestrial technology badly. They were even told to consider ramming the crafts if they felt like they could eject safely. The U.S. government wanted that technology before the Soviet Union could get its hands on it.

One such story involves two pilots who were on a training exercise from Eglin Air Force Base near Pensacola, Florida, in the panhandle. They were flying down to

One of the five Braxton County monster chairs situated throughout the county at key locations. *Photo by the author.*

MacDill Air Force Base in Tampa. This was on September 12, 1952. The official report notes that the pilot and trainee copilot were lost somewhere over the Gulf and never arrived at MacDill.

The families of the lost pilots were told that this was a training accident and nothing more. They were told that the plane was lost and that no bodies were recovered. Nearly forty years later, the families were told further details of the flight—that the men had made it to Tampa but, after quickly refueling, had relaunched and were then lost. There was no explanation for their relaunch.

Investigation into this tragic accident has led some to wonder if they were scrambled for their flight, as if there was a drill or a potential threat. There are some records from that day at MacDill that are heavily redacted. There are also some reports of a UFO sighted in the area from a civilian boat in Tampa Bay just before the recorded relaunch of the aircraft from MacDill.

The big questions linger: Were the two pilots scrambled to investigate the UFOs? Were they damaged or disabled from their encounter? Was it simply a freak accident? If so, why were they relaunched so quickly after landing from a long flight?

Frank Feschino thinks that these pilots engaged a UFO and damaged it. Tragically, they lost their lives doing so. The damaged craft would have continued nearly due north and slightly east. It could well have been the fiery ball in the sky seen by some boys in the town of Flatwoods, West Virginia, only a brief time later.

Fred and Edward May and their friend Eugene Lemon were playing football on the Flatwoods school playground with several other boys. They all saw a large glowing red object that was pear-shaped and had a flaming tail. It flew over their heads. At first, they thought it was a meteor until it suddenly came to a halt and then descended vertically. It landed on the farm of the Fisher family.

The May boys ran to their mother, Kathleen May, who took her boys and a few of the others to go to where the fiery thing had landed. It was giving off a red and purple light through the trees. They went with a few of the family dogs in tow.

Eugene Lemon was a National Guardsman, so he decided to lead the group up the steep hill to the Fisher farm, using his flashlight to lead the group through the forested area toward the eerie glow. The group suddenly noticed that they were engulfed in a warm mist that had a nausea-inducing odor. It was burning their eyes and made it exceedingly difficult to breathe.

One of the boys claimed that he heard a strange high-pitched mechanical whine at this point. One of the dogs growled and ran into the mist. It quickly came running back in fear and ran off back to town.

The boys and Mrs. May went on through the gate of the farm and up to the top of the hill, where the glow was coming from. The younger members of the group stayed back with one of the dogs, as it would not proceed any further.

The group that pressed ahead experienced an even stronger condensation of the mist, and the smell became even more unbearable. Mrs. May said that she could hear a strong hissing sound like bacon frying.

As they reached the top of the mountain, they saw a large, round metallic ball in a carved-out crevasse to their side just a short distance away. The black ball was large, and it was pulsing with a red and orange glow that seemed to cut through the dark exterior as though it was hollow.

Lemon then saw glowing eyes. At first, he had thought they were from a raccoon in a nearby tree. He brought his flashlight to the eyes and saw a dark "metal monster" standing nearly ten feet tall. It was lit from behind by a reddish glow, and the witnesses said the head or helmet was shaped like an ace of spades. The two eyes seemed to be like portholes with beams of glowing yellow light passing out of them. The creature suddenly came to life in the light.

The witnesses had varying descriptions of the strange creature's body. Some claimed that it had arms, while others said it was more like a bullet. Mrs. May famously described the body as looking like a pleated skirt made of metal. She did not see arms, but it had antennae coming from where it should have had shoulders.

It followed the flashlight beam toward them by gliding over the ground. The witnesses described a strange sound like a thump coming from the creature. It began to glow red in its face and green on the body. The hissing sound from earlier returned, and the strange foul-smelling mist seemed to swarm the group of terrified witnesses.

It came close to them, and Mrs. May said it launched an oily substance at them. At this point, they all turned and ran. They were convinced it was going to give chase, but it turned and went back toward the glowing ball. The group all fled to their homes.

Every one of the witnesses experienced nausea and severe nasal and throat issues. Lemon could not stop vomiting for a long period. Mrs. May took her children to a doctor, who claimed that the symptoms were similar to those affected by mustard gas in World War I.

The Flatwoods Monster based on the actual account of witnesses. The shoulders had antennae not arms. *Illustration by Kari Schultz.*

Mrs. May called the police as soon as she got home. The sheriff and his whole department were investigating a plane crash nearby, so they were unavailable. They sent a journalist named A. Lee Stewart Jr. to investigate and document the incident. He was there by 9:00 p.m. very shortly after the encounter.

Lemon led Stewart to the site. The journalist noticed the foul odor immediately and saw several strange tracks in the grass near the area where Lemon mentioned the creature had been spotted. He also noticed what looked like tractor marks on the ground (or perhaps military treads) leading down from where the glowing ball had been seen by Lemon and the witnesses.

Later, Stewart claimed to have found an unusual, oily material on his clothing. He would also claim to have found a blob-like lump of metal that had a similar consistency to solder. Stewart then interviewed all the witnesses and had them make drawings of the creature and the object. When the sheriff came later that night with a few police dogs, the animals refused to go anywhere near the location of the encounter.

Still later in the evening, the U.S. Air Force sent the West Virginia National Guard to investigate the scene. They were already in the area looking for a reported plane crash. Captain Dale Leavitt was in command of the investigation, and he told a local paper that they had found a metallic fragment and seemed to allege that locals may have taken some of the materials. He said that he hoped everyone would turn their materials over to the air force.

Leavitt would state later that he never did learn the results of any testing on the materials recovered or given to them after the fact. Either there was nothing to report or it was something classified higher than his clearance.

The next day, the May family were visited by two men who claimed to be reporters. She took them to the site. The men acted strangely and claimed something about bringing the samples to someone. They both wore very formal suits, and she was surprised that they seemed unconcerned about getting them covered in the black oily substance.

The papers ran the stories of UFOs for a few days and eventually the story of the encounter with the monster. The witnesses were talked to by many experts from various news outlets and publications. Mrs. May and Lemon posed for a famous photo at a New York TV station with an artist's rendering of the monster they had seen. This depiction is not what they had seen, but they went along with it.

The image from that photo is what many consider the "Flatwoods Monster." It took many liberties with the initial description. Many experts no longer consider it an accurate description.

Debunkers have claimed that the sighting was a meteor and that the glow was merely an airplane light that had fallen nearby from the plane crash that was found. The military presence was there for the crash. The

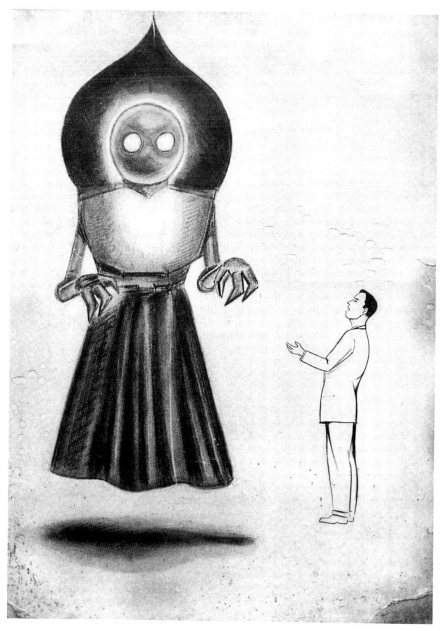

The illustration of the Flatwoods Monster as presented on New York Television news. *Image provided by Flatwoods Monster Museum.*

The wonderful displays at the Flatwoods Monster Museum in Sutton, West Virginia. *Photo by the author.*

monster was a barn owl spooked by the flashlight. The mist was a noxious gas from the meteor.

UFO landing cases were not common before this one made the news. They would become more prevalent a decade later in the 1960s, but they followed similar patterns to this one.

The Mays and all the witnesses were certain that they had seen something unusual that September night in Braxton County. It took years for the town of Flatwoods and nearby Sutton, West Virginia, to embrace their place in UFO lore. They felt, like so many others, that they would be made a laughingstock as the back-hills folk who saw an alien.

What is often overlooked in this case is that there was another sighting the next day in the nearby town of Frametown. A couple were on a drive through the mountains when their car stopped suddenly and would not start again. They smelled a putrid stench suddenly and got out of the car. They were looking to see what animal had died near them.

The couple instead saw a large creature before them. The body matched the description of the Flatwoods monster from the previous day. It was bullet-like with pleats of metal. However, the top was no longer in a suit. They described the creature as reptilian with yellow eyes and long scaly arms. It was like a gray alligator according to one of the witnesses.

The couple may have heard the story of the Braxton Monster, but it was not widely talked about and had not been in the papers at this point. They reported that they fled to their vehicle and were happy that it suddenly started. They were able to drive away quickly. It was only sometime later that the two stories seemed to combine, and people realized that this might have been the same creature.

The creature of that incident was known as the "Frametown Monster." It is now thought to be the same creature from Flatwoods. It has never been seen again.

Today, the county has five giant chairs decorated like "Braxxie" the monster. They are at key locations throughout the county. Tourists are encouraged to take pictures of all five. There is a great family restaurant called The Spot where you can eat a UFO calzone. It also sells iconic ceramic Flatwoods Monster lanterns made nearby. There is also now the Flatwoods Monster Museum in nearby Sutton, where many artifacts are on display, including some of the original sketches from the witnesses.

As for Frank Feschino, he is still digging for more evidence, as he has done for many years. He is convinced that there is still more to be told of this story.

PART II
PRE-1900

WIZARD CLIP

Middleway, West Virginia

In 1794, a solitary traveler stopped at the farm of Adam Livingston in the town of Middleway. As inns were not common in this period, farms often allowed guests to stay with them for a modest fee. The Livingston family welcomed the man and set him up in one of their guest rooms. The man was incredibly grateful as he was unwell and could travel no farther.

By the next day, he had worsened. He asked Adam to fetch a Roman Catholic priest, as he knew he was dying. He would need his last rites read to him. Livingston was a devout Lutheran and refused to do this—no Catholic priest would be allowed in his home.

The stranger succumbed to his illness and died. The family buried him unceremoniously on their farm with no religious service performed. This would prove to be a grave error on the Livingston family's part for their farm and the whole town of Middleway.

The home began to experience what we would now call poltergeist activity. Strange sounds like galloping of horses and poundings on the walls would echo throughout the farmhouse at all hours of the day and night. Money disappeared from hidden caches. The poultry outside began to suddenly lose their heads as if reaped by a great scythe. Logs would leap off the burning hearth and nearly burn the farmhouse to the ground.

Adam Livingston's memorial in Middleway on his donated land. *Image provided by the Priest Field Pastoral Center.*

That also led to the infamous "clipping." There would frequently be the sound of scissors snipping at cloth. Witnesses to the sound would suddenly find small crescent moon–shaped holes in their clothing, shoes or their bed linens. This was occurring at the Livingston farm as well as all throughout Middleway.

People would hear the telltale *snip snip* of the scissors. A check would reveal nearby leather or cloth cut with the moon-shaped holes no matter where it was stored or worn.

The small village of Middleway became known widely as "Wizard Clip." The townsfolk were suddenly famous as "Clippers." Tourists came from long distances to experience the strange phenomenon. The town was not exactly thrilled with the fame.

Famously, one grand lady of the nearby city of Martinsburg announced a trip to the Livingston farm itself to satisfy her curiosity. She removed her brand-new silk hat, wrapped it in a silk handkerchief and hid it in her pocket to hopefully avoid any damage. When she left, not only was her hat cut with the moon shapes, but her hankie and back of her dress were as well.

There are numerous documented cases of Livingston seeking help to alleviate the troubles besieging his farm and the town. His Lutheran pastor provided prayers and a vigil to no avail. A Methodist minister was brought to town and he had rocks thrown at him by some invisible force. A large rock once shot out of the chimney of the Livingston farmhouse chimney and spun on the floor for more than a quarter of an hour in front of several witnesses, including a German faith healer who had come to offer assistance.

Needless to say, the clipping and other activity still continued. Adam Livingston claimed to have had a strange dream about a robed man. He heard a booming voice say, "This is the man who can relieve you." Adam thought he recognized the man as Father Dennis Cahill in a nearby church.

Father Cahill was convinced to come to Middleway. He blessed the town and the farm. Instantly one of the missing caches of money returned. The Livingston family thought their troubles were over. This was not to be, and the strange occurrences returned after a brief respite. Father Cahill returned and performed a second blessing. The clipping stopped again for a time.

Adam Livingston eventually converted to Catholicism. He donated thirty acres of his land to support a new priest for the town. There is some

This large cross is a dedication to the stranger who was the origin of the Wizard Clip phenomenon. *Image provided by the Priest Field Pastoral Center.*

Signs in the area denote the Wizard Clip incident with scissors and a half moon on them. *Image provided by the Appalachian Folklore Depository.*

controversy as to whether he and his wife were willing converts. The donation is still valid to this day. The land is now called the Priest's Field.

Priest Field Pastoral Center is a retreat for Catholics, complete with a chapel and a grand dining hall. There are meeting rooms and guest rooms and apartments for visitors. It has a beautiful garden and lies along lazy Opequon Creek.

Adams Livingston's donation now hosts groups as diverse as Alcoholics Anonymous and psychic mediums. People of all kinds of beliefs and religions are welcome to use the center's facilities. Several nonprofits from all over bring people here for quiet getaways.

Priest Field director Susan Kersey said of her workplace, "This is very special holy ground. There are lots of nooks and crannies here. Let the Lord show you how important you are…the Lord loves each of you and there's a place for you. It's all about healing and going forth."

There are still some people who claim to hear the *snip snip* sounds in the town off and on to this very day. Interestingly, the town avoided much modernization and is home to wonderful older buildings that have been around since before the Wizard Clip days. It is a great place to travel back in time in the panhandle of West Virginia.

SERPENT MOUND, ALLIGATOR MOUND AND THE CROSSWICK SERPENT

Ohio River Valley

As much as we know about the history of the Appalachians and its inhabitants, surprisingly little is truly known about the indigenous tribes of the areas. Many of the tribes left little trace of their existence. Others left an impossible-to-miss sign of their passing. These were the Mound Builders.

Ohio, West Virginia and Kentucky are well known for many of their Mound Builder sites. They are well maintained today, but this was not always the case. As settlers moved into these states after passing through the Appalachian Mountains, they were overwhelmed with the sheer number of these earthen structures. Ohio alone had more than one thousand known mounds.

These historic sites were mostly used as landmarks or simple curiosity locations to the early settlers. Sadly, as land became more and more scarce and valuable, many of these sites were destroyed.

There has been much investigative research done of this period. People discovered that there were primarily two forms of earthworks created by the Mound Builders. First were the burial mounds. These appear to have been the oldest structures. They are also the easiest to be dated, as they had artifacts and bodies at their base.

Similar to the pyramids half a world away in Egypt, the smaller mounds would have one burial chamber that would be filled with valuables and artifacts. The larger mounds had fewer artifacts but many more burial chambers. Speculation among archaeologists and anthropologists believe that the more important people commanded the single smaller mounds to account for the discrepancy with the treasures lain with them.

The second type of mound is harder to understand. These earthworks have nothing stored within them. Many are shaped into effigies of animals. Archaeologists again suspect that these were place markers for points of historical, religious or political significance among the Mound Builders. Some align with celestial events similar to Stonehenge in England. Most remain a mystery in purpose.

The Mound Builders have been classified into three basic divisions in the area. The divisions span more than two thousand years. By AD 1200, they had all either left the area or had simply stopped creating earthworks. Studies indicate that the culture may have come to some abrupt end. We will most likely never know what happened to them.

The three cultures of Mound Builders are named for areas where they were discovered. They are the Adena Culture, the Hopewell Culture and the Fort Ancient Culture. The cultures were found all over along the major rivers and in many mountain passes. They are in greater numbers as the lands flatten out beyond the mountains.

The three divisions do not mean that they were three different tribes. Rather, they had three major cycles of their society—like our changes from an agrarian society into a post–industrial revolution modernization. It is possible they were three different tribes, but many consider that unlikely. Rather, it is thought they were one people evolving and changing their culture.

Among the earthworks of these people is an effigy mound called Alligator Mound in Granville, Ohio. The mound is more than two hundred feet long and six feet high at its highest point. It is on top of a bluff overlooking Raccoon Creek Valley. When viewed from above, it resembles a four-legged animal with a round head and curled tail.

Since it is close to the Newark Earthworks, it is originally thought to be of the Hopewell Culture. Recent studies, however, have suggested that it was built by the later Fort Ancient Culture. As noted, effigy mounds are difficult to date even today.

Early settlers said that the natives of the area called it "Alligator Mound" and so the name stuck even though the earthworks look nothing like an alligator. There are also not many alligators in Ohio. We do know that the Calusa tribe in what is now Miami, Florida, traded with some of the early tribes of this area due to some basalt axe heads that had come from this

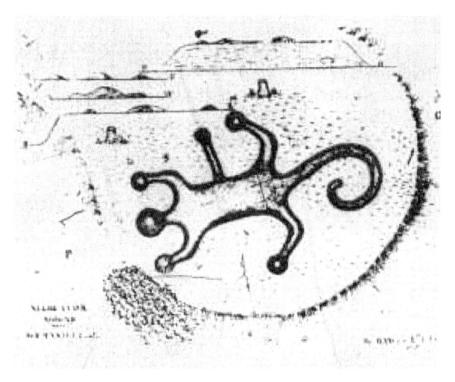

An early map of Alligator Mound from archaeologists intent on discovering more of its origins. *Image provided by Ohio Mound Builder Historical Society.*

area and were discovered in the Miami Mystery Circle. It is possible that the name might have meant something.

The more likely reason was hypothesized by archaeologist Brad Leffer in the early 2000s. He believes that the mound is a depiction of Mishipeshu, the Underwater Panther.

Among the woodland tribes and even the Great Lakes tribes, the Underwater Panther is one of the great creatures of their beliefs, particularly among the water powers. The Ojibwe tribe and the Anishinaabe people speak of the creature often in their tales and teachings.

Mishipeshu is often translated as the "Great Lynx." It is a mixture of many creatures in its description. It has the head of a giant cat but is covered in scales. It has spiked spines like an alligator down its back to its long circular tail. The beast has great claws like a bear. It is a fearsome creature to behold and rules the rivers and large lakes.

The Algonquin tribe believed the Underwater Panther to be the most powerful of all the underworld creatures. The Ojibwes were convinced that it was the master of all snakes and water creatures. Nearly all tribes believed it to be in opposition to the Great Thunderbirds that ruled the skies and the Great Serpent that ruled the underworld.

The stories claim that the creature always lives in the deepest parts of lakes and rivers. The creature can cause great whirlpools with its tail. Its roar can bring great storms. Some stories claim it to be benevolent, but most describe it as a powerful, evil force. It could be calmed, however, with offerings and sacrifices.

Famously, a Jesuit missionary named Claude Dablon spoke of a story from some Ojibwa natives. A group of warriors had gone to an island that was the home of Mishipeshu to grab copper for their home. The natives had long mined copper along the Ohio Valley and the Great Lakes. They said that the minute they left the island, Mishipeshu attacked them for stealing his children's shiny toys. Most of the warriors were slain on the spot, with one returning to warn the others as he perished.

Pictographs of the Underwater Panther look much closer to the design of Alligator Mound than an actual alligator. The name Alligator Mound may come from early settlers describing the Underwater Panther. The settlers would think, "There is no such thing as an Underwater Panther, but a spiky-tailed creature that lives underwater and kills people? That sounds like an alligator." This is the theory proposed by Brad Leffer.

The largest earthwork in North America is Serpent Mound. It is believed to represent the Great Serpent, which rules the underworld. The Great

Serpent Mound as viewed from the air is the only way to truly appreciate the size of this amazing structure. *Image provided by Ohio Mound Builder Historical Society.*

Serpent appears in many Native American beliefs. He is usually associated with the underworld, lightning and death.

Among the Cherokees, the Great Serpent is known as Uktena. He was also venerated by the Choctaws, the Chickasaws, the Creeks and several other tribes. Many believe the great serpent to be invisible and that it brought the rains. Others say that it is the reason for earthquakes. It is depicted as having one great eye on the top of its head. Sometimes it has horns in pictograms.

According to the Sioux, the great water monsters, the Unktehila, lived long ago, and the Thunderbirds destroyed them. The Thunderbird legends may have been inspired by pterosaur skulls and the great serpents being killed by them from the various dinosaur skeletons discovered.

Serpent Mound is in north Adams County, Ohio. It is an amazing site to behold. It is an effigy mound that represents an uncoiling snake along the top of a ridge. It is 1,427 feet in length, which would be similar in size to lying the Empire State Building beside it. When it was originally detailed in 1848 by early archaeologists, the main body of the mound was described as being 5 feet high, with a width of 25 feet.

In the late 1880s, Fredric Putnam of Harvard University dug trenches into the earthwork to reveal its structure. He found no cultural artifacts to date it. It was assumed to be of the Adena Culture due to two Adena burial mounds located nearby. However, there is also a Fort Ancient Culture burial mound there as well. Recent excavations tend to add credence to people from the Fort Ancient Culture being the ones who built it.

The head of serpent mound is aligned with the setting sun of the summer solstice. The coils appear to be aligned with other equinoxes or solstices.

Early explorers thought that the great serpent's head looked like it was eating an apple. As Christianity shows the devil as a snake tempting man with the apple, they thought this was a sign that Christianity had been worshiped by the early tribes. Now we see it looks more like that the serpent depicted had a large singular eye, as the Great Serpent of the Native American creature of the underworld. Serpent Mound should probably be called the Great Serpent Mound.

Fredric Putnam famously saved Serpent Mound from destruction. Harvard University, with his help, funded the purchase of the historical site. The area was turned into a public park until it was transferred to the Ohio State Archaeological Society in 1900. In 1908, the first observation tower was built to see the whole of the serpent from above. It is now a National Historic Landmark, as is Alligator Mound.

Mishipeshu, the underwater panther, is very similar to the Crosswick Serpent descriptions. *Illustration by Kari Schultz.*

The question becomes: Did Mishipeshu and the Great Serpent exist other than in beliefs and myths? We have one documented encounter that might bring these creatures into a more modern era.

On the banks of the Miami River in Warren County, Ohio, not far from Alligator Mound, a small town called Crosswick had an unforgettable encounter with something out of a nightmare in 1882.

Two young boys were fishing in a small creek that led into the river. A large monster with reptilian features, looking like a great demon, charged at them. It grabbed the older boy in a mighty clawed hand and ran away toward a large sycamore tree. It crawled into a hole at the base with the boy. The younger boy ran for help.

Some men nearby heard the screams and came running over. Soon the whole town was worked into a furor, and more than sixty men went to save the boy from the mighty beast. They began to chop at the tree with axes. As they struck, the creature emerged from its hiding spot and released the boy. It raced away faster than a horse, according to the witnesses. It ran up a hill and over a fence. It ran for more than a mile before scrambling into another hole under a rocky outcropping.

The creature, as seen in the open, was described as being forty feet long. It was never mentioned to be a dinosaur, even though the word was becoming common in that period. It was described as a great snake with arms and legs. It also propelled itself with its tail. This was in stark contrast to the view of dinosaurs of the period, when it was thought they dragged their tails behind them.

The story claims that the creature retreated into the earth and was never seen again. Did the people of Crosswick have an encounter with a remaining dinosaur, or did they encounter Mishipeshu or one of the children of the Great Serpent?

PART III

HAUNTED HOT SPOTS

THE KIRKBRIDE ASYLUMS: TRANS-ALLEGHENY, WAVERLY HILLS, PENHURST AND THE RIDGES

In the nineteenth century, there were tremendous advancements in the treatment of the mentally ill in the United States. State funding began to be opened to assist with the issue. Activists and doctors pushed for more humane treatments. New therapies were being developed throughout the world. There became a huge push for public institutions to treat the growing number of newly diagnosed patients.

The money was now readily available for public "lunatic asylums." These facilities would replace previous methods of dealing with the mentally ill. Usually, people were placed in prisons or poorhouses. They were often abused, and their needs were rarely met.

The most influential man for the premise of the asylum system was Dr. Thomas Story Kirkbride. He published a paper on asylum design and intended function. These detailed principles would influence the construction and handling of many asylums built throughout America in this period. Kirkbride felt that the asylum itself would be integral to the treatment plan for the patients.

Throughout Appalachia, there were several asylums built according to the Kirkbride Plan. Dr. Thomas Story saw the asylum as a place of structured activities and seclusion from illnesses. He felt that certain amounts of medical therapy were necessary as well. The plan intended

Trans-Allegheny Lunatic Asylum is being continuously restored. It is a prime example of a Kirkbride hospital. *Photo by the author.*

to provide an overall improvement to the welfare and care for the patients and improve the quality of life for society as a whole.

Kirkbride planned his asylums like the wings of a bat. A central administration building would house the staff and care facilities. Two wings would stretch out from there. Female patients would be housed in one wing and male in the other. Each wing would then be divided based on how "excited" the patients were. Those being the worst would be placed on the lower floors and farthest from the administration building. "Calmer" patients would be placed on the upper floors and closer to the center.

This plan was meant to make the patients' stays more comfortable and productive. You could avoid being antagonized by other patients that might affect your treatment. Fresh air, natural light and well-tended grounds were all part of the plan to help heal damaged psyches.

These asylums were generally placed a distance from any nearby cities. They would be free from pollution and urban sprawl. The need for fresh outdoor air and promotion of a cheerful atmosphere at all times would help in every conceivable way for treatment. Kirkbride was certain of this.

Most of the Kirkbride asylums would be built with farms. The patients could help tend the gardens and fields. It made the asylums far more self-sufficient. The patients could also participate in other chores around the asylum to give them a sense of purpose and responsibility. All the while it would be stimulating the patients' minds with calm and natural beauty.

Kirkbride promoted the plan for his entire life. As the twentieth century dawned, people began to lose faith in the system. A lack of evidence of permanently cured patients and no reduction in the number of patients being admitted became huge factors among public discourse. States began cutting funding to the asylums with no reduction in the incidences of mental illness.

As psychoanalysis and new drug treatments began, asylums were on the path to obsolescence. Kirkbride buildings were no longer built. Many were closed over the course of the next century. Many of the asylums were transformed into state hospitals or government centers. Many were used well into the 1980s.

Each of the asylums has a unique history. Sadly, many of these hospitals were stigmatized in general due to several key facilities being overcrowded and losing their funding. Public outcry began to outweigh the benefits of the old facilities. Many were deteriorating in general, with costly renovations continually being pushed back. Scandals of abuse and unsanitary conditions ran rampant. Many of the facilities were demolished, as the cost to renovate them would have been exorbitant.

To this day there are many that still are in danger of being demolished. With city expansions and land costs skyrocketing, even more are threatened with imminent destruction all in the name of progress.

Now there are always stories of hauntings and unusual activities at these locations. Famously, the Ridges in Athens, Ohio, formerly known as the Athens Lunatic Asylum, once held an exorcism for a fourteen-year-old girl suffering from epilepsy. Her ghost supposedly haunts the main building. This building sat vacant for a number of years. It was saved from destruction by Ohio University. It remodeled much of the Ridges; it now houses some of its administration and even an art collection.

The Ridges was one of the longest-running Kirkbride asylums. It operated from 1874 to 1993. The nearby cemeteries house more than 1,900 graves. Most were buried and marked only with a number on their stone. In recent years, there are groups attempting to provide names on the stones for families to reclaim their loved ones.

In one of the rooms on the top floor of the ridges lies a stain in the concrete that has never been able to be cleaned. A patient named Margaret Schilling

Above: The Athens Lunatic Asylum was empty for a long period. It deteriorated quickly. This image was from the period after it had been abandoned for a few years. *Image provided by the Ridges.*

Left: The Ridges, as of now, are nearly fully restored and house the offices of Ohio University. *Image provided by Ohio University.*

Inside the halls of Trans-Allegheny Lunatic Asylum, you never know what you might find among the ghosts of the past. *Photo by the author.*

died there in 1979. She supposedly had hidden herself from the staff and died there. It appears now that she had locked herself in an unused wing of the hospital and died of exposure. Her ghost supposedly haunts the room where she died. The stain is still visible today.

The Trans-Allegheny Asylum in Weston, West Virginia, is a favorite among paranormal investigators, as it allows private tours for a fee. Every dollar made goes back into restoring the facility as a landmark for this period in mental healthcare. The building hosts tours daily that range from historic to those focusing on the paranormal aspects of the former hospital.

Trans-Allegheny was one of the most notorious of the overcrowded facilities. It was swarmed with patients and was severely underfunded by the state. It had been considered one of the out-of-sight, out-of-mind hospitals with the state. It was also the home of the most lobotomy surgeries among all the Kirkbride hospitals. Paranormal investigators claim that it is rife with activity.

Penhurst Asylum in Spring City, Pennsylvania, is another infamous Kirkbride. It is a sprawling complex of buildings that covers hundreds of

Pennhurst Asylum as it appears today. *Image provided by Pennhurst Restoration Society.*

acres. It was shuttered in 1987, and patients are frequently seen still on the grounds, long after it had closed, as they had nowhere else to go. Most notably here are the extensive tunnels that were built to transport patients and materials under the ground between buildings to not upset the clean and calm grounds for the patients.

Penhurst was purchased by a group dedicated to its preservation. Randy Bates of the Bates Motel Haunted Attraction was allowed to turn parts of Pennhurst into a haunted attraction itself starting in the early 2000s. They use the money made to invest into the facilities to save the buildings they can. It, too, is frequented by paranormal experts for ghost tours. Eager investigators are encouraged to explore the tunnel system.

Waverly Hills is considered by many to be the most haunted of all the Kirkbride asylums. Located outside Louisville, Kentucky, the asylum had been semi-successful in treating the mentally ill as originally intended. When tuberculosis became an epidemic, patients from all over Kentucky and Ohio were sent to Waverly for treatment. The hospital was overwhelmed. Many died as treatment was simply not available. Waverly was simply a large hospice care unit in addition to trying to treat the mentally unstable.

Waverly Hills Sanitarium is now home to a haunted attraction every year as well. It also runs paranormal tours throughout the rest of the year. While no attempts are being made to restore the grand building, money is being used to preserve it and to prevent further disrepair.

Top: Waverly Hills Sanitarium stands ominously in the hills just outside Louisville, Kentucky. *Image provided by Eastern Kentucky Paranormal.*

Bottom: Radar Hill Cemetery, where a large number of patients from the Athens Lunatic Asylum are buried. *Photo by the author.*

Although each hospital has a grand history of both tragedy and triumph, it should be noted that Dr. Kirkbride had the best of intentions. Aside from the issues caused by overcrowding and lack of funding, these facilities offered a lot of good for their patients in the early days of mental healthcare. Sadly, their dark histories sometimes overshadow the positives.

SCREAMING JENNY

Moulton, Alabama

Louisa Elisabeth Jane Bates was born on January 22, 1826, in the hills of Kentucky. At the age of fourteen, she married Willis Brooks Jr., a man some twenty years her senior. He was a saddle maker and leather worker. Jane was a beauty to behold according to all who knew her. She was half Cherokee and had deep-blue eyes. The couple were reportedly very happy together.

The Brooks family had many children and eventually moved to Alabama. There they operated a popular inn at a crossroads of serval main routes through the state at the foothills of the southwestern tip of the Appalachian Mountains. The inn was right on the main throughway to the Mississippi River ports. They were doing quite well for themselves.

Then the Civil War broke out. Alabama in their area had little love for the war. They felt that it was a rich man's war. After the initial rush of recruitment in the early days of the war, the Confederacy started having issues meeting the need for soldiers. So, it created a draft. The draft caused further resentment, as the rich cold pay others to fight in their stead or were granted exemptions if they owned more than twenty slaves.

It was widely believed that Willis Brooks was acting as a spy at his inn for the Union in the North. At the very least, he publicly advocated for neutrality. Word got out to a band of the Confederate Home Guard about his sympathies. The Home Guard were primarily enforcers of the draft, but they also acted as tax collectors. They came to the inn of the Brooks family sometime in late 1863. They forced Willis Brooks out of his inn and prepared to lynch him on a nearby tree. They brought out his wife, Jane, and all their children to watch the act.

The eldest son of the family grabbed a gun from the house, intent on saving his father. Instead, he was gunned down before he could fire. The Guardsmen then hanged Willis Brooks. When he did not die quickly enough for their taste, they shot him as well. They then left the grieving family and went away.

Jane grabbed all of her children and brought them to the bodies of her husband and her eldest son. She made the rest of her children put their hands on the blood of their fallen kin. She then made them swear a Cherokee blood oath to not rest until every member of that gang of Confederate Guard had been slain in the name of vengeance.

Jane took the name of "Aunt Jenny." She was a young widow with a baby and several young children to care for. She kept to the inn but also taught the children how to fight. She would say in later years that she "wasted many a keg of powder teaching my boys to shoot!"

The eight men were hunted over the years after, and five of them were killed by her children. Two more were slain by Jenny herself. The men were found in various locations from Texas all the way back to Kentucky. It took many years, and many of the sons of the Willis family died in the attempts to hunt their father's murderers.

In the years that followed, Aunt Jenny would marry again. She also bore a few more children. Her previous children had become legends in their own right and fought with various gangs. Famously, there was a rivalry with the Hubbard family that rivaled the Hatfield/McCoy feud in body count alone. When one of her sons was killed in a gunfight where he was ambushed by twenty men, she was pleased to hear he had taken six of them with him.

After her last son, Henry, had died, Jenny was famously quoted as saying, "All of my sons died like men. They all had their boots on." About all the feuds and gang fights over the years involving her family, she said, "After that terrible night we were never going to let anyone get the better of us again."

The family never found the last of the Confederate Guard. Jenny lived to be ninety-eight years old. As she lay on her deathbed, she asked her priest to bring a soap dish to her that she had made herself many years ago. She wanted to wash away the blood and the sin on her hands. He brought it to her. She washed her hands and then passed away.

As the priest went to put the dish away, he noticed it was of an odd shape. After close examination, he realized what it was. Jenny had made the dish from the skull of the first man that they had killed in retribution for the death of her first husband.

Jenny apparently still haunts the Appalachian foothills of Alabama. Her ghost is seen still hunting the last of the Guard who escaped her. She shouts an unearthly scream at witnesses. She is known as "Screaming Jenny" in the hills. Everyone says that she is a spirit of red glowing shadow, except for her piercing blue eyes.

THE MOONVILLE TUNNEL

Vinton County, Ohio

In one of the densest woods in eastern Ohio lies the town of Moonville. In 1856, the Marietta-Cincinnati Railroad was trying to build a line in through southeastern Ohio. A man named Samuel Coe had a coal mine in the middle of these wooded hills and heard of the railroad line's need.

Coe offered much of his land to the railroad company for free. All he asked was that a stop be placed so he could load coal and clay from his mine. The railroad was overjoyed at the offer, and it would connect to Cincinnati with a greatly reduced travel time even with the added stop. More stops would also be added for fueling and other services along the new rail line.

One of the towns that sprang up along the line was Moonville. It was named for the town's general store operator, who was named Mr. Moon. Moonville also had its own coal mine and famously supplied coal for nearby Hope Furnace. The town had gown to a small community of nearly one hundred residents by 1870.

Moonville Tunnel is now accessible once again for visitors. The bridge over Racoon Creek leads to this site of so many deaths. *Photo by the author.*

The Baltimore & Ohio Railroad purchased the line in the 1880s. While this increased rail traffic, it did not help the towns along the way. Stops became less frequent. The mines near Moonville had run mostly dry by this time. By the early 1900s, the town began to dwindle to nothing.

The last family left Moonville in 1947. The buildings were all gone by the late 1960s. The line itself was abandoned in the 1980s. The only remnants of the town were a tunnel, the town cemetery and a few old telegraph poles.

Now the old rail line has been converted into a wilderness trail for hiking and horseback riding. The old train trestle bridge just past the tunnel was demolished and replaced with a footbridge. The tunnel itself is a marvel to behold and has numerous ghost stories for a town that had such a short life itself.

The most famous story involves a drunk brakeman coming home through the tunnel after a night playing poker. A train hit the tunnel, and the brakeman vainly swung his light to try to stop it as the tunnel is so narrow; he had nowhere to go. He was decapitated.

The ghost of the brakeman was reported numerous times and is said to haunt the tunnel to this day. People see his light swinging back and forth. The Baltimore & Ohio rail line did, in fact, install a signal at the Moonville tunnel in 1981. There were numerous trains emergency breaking as they entered the tunnel due to seeing strange waving lights. Engineers were instructed to ignore any lights in that tunnel other than the main light outside the tunnel.

A second ghost is often spotted in the tunnel. A young woman was coming to visit her fiancé in Moonville. She had walked the whole way from her hometown and was crossing the trestle bridge over Raccoon Creek just before the tunnel. She was struck by a train on the bridge. Her ghost is often seen wandering the bridge looking for her lost love.

Yet another ghost is seen in the tunnel. This may be the oldest ghost there. One of the earliest trains coming through the newly built tunnel stopped just outside the tunnel after crossing the trestle. The conductor was apparently having an affair with the engineer's wife. The engineer had found out about this.

As the train stopped, the engineer asked the conductor to check the break line. As the conductor climbed under the train to check, the engineer hit the throttle and ended the conductor's life. Some versions of the story say that this was simply an accident. We do know that there were reported sightings of the apparition of the conductor as far back as 1890.

The town itself was no stranger to deaths over the years. The graveyard marks the death of a man who fell asleep on the tracks and was run over several times. One man crossed the tracks after waiting for a train to pass only to be killed when an uncoupled car hit him when he assumed it to be clear to cross the tracks. The last recorded death was in 1986, when a young girl was killed on the trestle bridge by a CSX train.

There is another legend about the bridge. It claims that the young lady who died looking for her love will bless the bond of your love if you place a lock on the old trestle bridge with your names on it. When visiting the tunnel, you will see dozens of locks with names attached to the fence of the bridge as you cross Raccoon Creek. It is not recommended, as the state is deciding how often to come and remove them.

The drive to the tunnel is on a very thin road through dense forest even today. It is an amazing drive, but make certain to download any directional maps, as the signal is easily lost and there is no one for miles to assist you, except maybe a few ghosts from Moonville.

THE GREENBRIAR GHOST

Lewisburg, West Virginia

A young boy who did chores for the Shue family came into their home on January 23, 1897. At the bottom of the stairs, he found the body of Elva Zona Heaster Shue lying dead. The boy, Andy Jones, ran for help and returned to his home.

Andy found his mother and informed her of his dark discovery. He then went to inform the husband, Edward S. Shue, of the tragic news. Edward was working as at the blacksmith shop and was noted to be in great anguish when he heard the news.

Edward ran home and held the body of his poor dead wife. Dr. George W. Knapp was the local doctor, and he also acted as the coroner. Edward would not let his dead wife out of his arms while the doctor conducted his examination of the body. Knapp concluded that she had "died of an everlasting faint." We would now most likely call that a heart attack.

The body was prepared for burial, and again Edward insisted on helping with the preparation of the body, as he was so distraught for her loss. Dr. Knapp noted how tenderly he always held her head. He placed several cloth items around her head to help her rest easier. He also tied a large

The grave of the Greenbriar Ghost.
Photo by the author.

scarf around her neck, saying that it had always been her favorite.

The body of Zona was brought for display to the home of her mother, Mrs. Mary Jane Heaster. She lived on nearby Big Sewell Mountain. When the casket was on display, Shue remained at the head during the viewing. Zona was buried at the cemetery on the hill. Everyone mourned the loss of the young woman, but it was considered just a tragic death of one too young.

A few weeks passed, and Mrs. Heaster began to tell her friends that she had been visited by the spirit of her dead daughter. She said that Edward had been a cruel and violent husband. He had attacked her in a rage and broken her neck. She also claimed that Edward was really a man called "Trout."

Mary and her brother-in-law went to Lewisburg prosecutor John Preston. He completely disbelieved her story. After several hours of her insistence, Preston began to feel that there was a need for an investigation.

Dr. Knapp was called, and he admitted that he might have been wrong in his diagnosis of the cause of Zona's death. He remarked on the unusual care Edward had taken with the body's head and neck.

Further investigation showed that Edward Shue may have been named Erasmus Stribbling Shue, otherwise known as "Trout." He had two previous wives, and both had died under mysterious circumstances. His first wife died of a broken neck when she fell from a haystack. The second wife died while assisting Shue with the repair of a chimney in their home. He had dropped a rock onto her head while at a great height, seemingly by accident.

The prosecutor was convinced and ordered an exhumation of the body. It was noted that Edward "Trout" Shue complained vociferously about the procedure. He was informed that there would be an inquest; if he did not go willingly, he would be forced to come. He was quoted as saying, "I know I'll be arrested, but they will not be able to prove I did it."

The autopsy provided the proof needed for conviction. Zona's neck was indeed broken, and her windpipe was smashed in. On her throat were finger marks from where she had been choked to death.

The historical marker sign for the Greenbriar Ghost. *Photo by the author.*

The community became enraged when the findings were made public. Shue was arrested and charged with murder. On June 22, 1897, the jury found him guilty of the crime after a very brief deliberation. The newspapers made it a point to show that it was the discovery of his history and not a "ghost's testimony" that led to his conviction.

Shue was sentenced to life in prison. There was an attempt to lynch him, but it was foiled by local law enforcement. He was taken to Moundsville State Prison, where he would later die in 1900.

There is a state highway marker a few miles away from Zona's grave that summarizes her story well:

> *Interred in a nearby cemetery is Zona Heaster Shue. Her death in 1897 was presumed natural until her spirit appeared to her mother to describe how she was killed by her husband Edward. Autopsy on the exhumed body verified the apparition's account. Edward, found guilty of murder, was sentenced to state prison.*
>
> *This remains the only documented case where a ghost was involved with solving their own murder.*

PART IV

EVERY HOLLER HAS A CREATURE

An Introduction to Holler Life

For those not raised in Appalachia, I have decided to explain what a holler is and a little about those who live there. The basic definition is that it's a lane or road that follows a narrow valley between a set of hills. If you are from a holler, you know there is a lot more to a holler than that simple definition.

Most hollers do not even have fully paved roads. Many are mostly dirt roads with a bit of gravel on them here and there. Hollers are usually very sparsely populated, as that is what most of those who live there prefer. They guard their privacy and are very wary of strangers. Usually there is not one house in sight of another along the road.

As wary as they are of outsiders, they are fiercely loyal to one another as neighbors. When someone needs help, someone will help. If someone gets seriously ill in the holler, other neighbors will help until they get better. Once you are accepted into a holler community, you will have the most loyal group to have your back outside of blood family.

There usually are not any fancy homes in a holler. Most are modest, and almost everyone has a barn of some sort. Most have other outbuildings. Mostly these are not large farms, but there will usually be chickens, cows, goats and a few horses around. There is always at least one dog that will run up and down the road barking at every car that comes by.

Most homes in the holler will have a front porch that people actually use. They will sit on it and shell peas and green beans. Other people will come by and sit on the porch with you. There will be discussions about crooked politicians and the latest community gossip. In the evenings, someone will bring out a fiddle, guitar or banjo and will make the sweetest, most amazing music you have ever heard. Sometimes you can hear the music miles down the holler.

The bulk of the houses in these hollers have been occupied by several generations of the same family. They play in the same creek their grandmother used to wash clothes in. Being in the house where your father was born brings an amazing sense of comfort. They never feel alone, as they have ancestor after ancestor buried in the nearby hills. There is a serenity to knowing a personal family history with the land.

Living in a holler, you will never ever be truly alone. You will always get recognition from those around you. People always wave when they see you on the porch or in the front yard. If they do not see you, then they will blow their horn when they drive by your house. This is just a way to let you know they are thinking of you. If a few days pass and no one sees you, they will come by to check on you. You can count on them, and they expect to count on you.

There is, however, a code that must be followed by those who live there. The first house as you drive into the holler is called the mouth. The job of those at the mouth is to keep a wary eye. If they see a strange car that does not belong, then they call the people who live behind them and let them know that a stranger is heading into the holler. If a salesperson or government representative comes to the door, their job is to call the neighbors so the big dogs can be let out farther up the holler. They are the sentries.

The homes at the end of the holler are the bug-out points. They have the best tornado cellars. They have the biggest guns for hunting. They are also the ones on the edge of the forests and mountains. Their job is to keep the stories of the spirits and legends of the holler alive for the next generation. Sometimes it is their job to make the right offerings to the spirits of the hills.

There are unwritten rules of the hollers. If a fire breaks out, everyone helps. If there is flooding, everyone makes certain everyone else is safe. When the snows or severe storms come through, everybody pitches in to make sure everyone can handle the dangers.

The hills will cradle you to sleep. They will protect you. A holler is where you will be safe. Once welcomed into a community, you will never find a place with more of a sense of belonging. You will be home. That said, nearly every holler has its own share of legends and stories. Most never pass beyond the mouth of the holler. Some grow and take on a life all their own once out of their area of origin. This is how creatures like the

Jersey Devil grow and become internationally famous. For generations, the stories rarely left home, as they feared they would be ridiculed like those folks in Flatwoods or Hopkinsville.

The families did not think them less real—they just did not spread the stories beyond the holler. Offerings were still left for the little people, just as their ancestors had since they settled in the valley. Rules were still followed about not answering strange voices from the hills. The "Hide-Behind" and the "Seek-N-Hide" are always looking for their next victim. You honor your ancestors and your kin by keeping the old stories alive by firelight.

The following pages are full of stories that were shared to us over e-mails, phone calls and in-person interviews over the last few years. Some were told based on total anonymity. Others were sent freely after hearing us on a podcast or seeing us on a show. Many were told to us as we toured, signing our previous books. All are printed with permission from the original tellers.

While not anywhere near a comprehensive list of holler legends, we have tried to bring forth a wide variety of these accounts. Where able, we tried to dig into the history of many of them. In honesty, that is beyond the scope of this book and may very well be another project in the future.

Some stories may seem familiar to similar tales from overseas. Many will fall into one of several categories. We have tried to summarize them for brevity as they were told to us. Part of the fun is hearing the tales from an original source. We highly suggest seeking your own tales on trips throughout Appalachia. With the current fascination with Bigfoot and Mothman in the world, it is now easier than ever to learn of these amazing creatures outside of a holler environment.

That said, the holler folk are still as protective of their own as always. If they doubt your sincerity, you are just as likely to be taken on a snipe hunt as a hunt for something more substantial. Like always, do not poke the bear. If a legend has rules that you should never break, DON'T BREAK THEM! You have been warned!

THE BONE LADY

Amqui, Quebec

Near where the Appalachians meet the Atlantic in the Great White North, they have their share of holler monster stories. Most famously are the tales of Wendigo. It is a Native American legend of a cursed creature that was once a human who committed the unspeakable crime of cannibalism. They are forced to live their undead lives as a skin-walker and shape-changing creature that must hunt forever and will never be able to satiate their hunger.

There is, however, one whose crimes were so great she was turned into something far worse. This local baby-minder helped the families of the local fishermen and huntsmen. She would take care of the children who were too young for school. The local families were so thankful for her services. Every able-bodied person was needed during the hot summer days to bring in as much harvest as possible.

Mother Tabitha was always welcome in every home for providing such a service. She would feast with a different family every night and was as welcome as the local school matron. She was also sadly without children of her own. The town cared for her as she tended to the smallest children.

The winters were harsh and the summers sometimes brutal. Occasionally, one of the children would succumb to some sort of illness or accident. The families and the whole community would grieve and then move on, as time was always against them. No one seemed to notice the unusually high mortality rate among the younger children until it became a bit more obvious as the numbers grew.

One of the older children went to get his youngest brother from Mother Tabitha one day and observed her dancing naked with a caribou-headed monster while the children sat entranced nearby. He ran and told his parents. They led a group of townsfolk to investigate this incident. Once there, they learned that another child had expired from a strange sickness. They confronted Mother Tabitha with the evidence.

She shrieked and fled into the woods. Under her dress, they saw that she was a creature made entirely of the bones of children. Only her head was human. It appeared that after each child was buried, she would dig it up and eat its corpse. She was hunted down and destroyed by holy water and a sacrament at the stone structure her and her wendigo mate had been cornered in. The families mourned, and the children took days to break from their trance-like state.

Some of the older families in the area still refuse to allow anyone to babysit their children.

THE DEVIL SPIDER

Hudson Valley, New York

In the early 1920s, a family in New York State tells a tale of exploring their inherited farmland from the early 1800s. They found a forgotten barn that had been nearly reclaimed by nature. There was no record of this barn on their property, so it had to predate the family ownership. As they approached it, they noticed a large number of skeletal remains of animals nearby. Fearing that poachers were using the barn for a base of activity, they approached with caution.

Once in the barn, the family could not believe the sheer number of cobwebs strewn through the nearly collapsed barn. It was obvious that no one had been in here for years. One of the younger boys mentioned that the spider webs were as strong as steel; they were unable to cut through some of them.

As they disturbed the webbing, dozens of dog-sized spiders came pouring out of the seemingly endless tunnels of cobwebs. The youngest boy noted that one of them was as tall as he was. A great creaking of the wooden frame of the barn was then heard by all. The family had already begun to run back to the entrance.

The father then turned and saw a giant spider leg as tall as a horse come out of the webbing as he slammed the door to the old barn shut. Fearing for his family's life, he ran to the car and got a can of gas. He lit the barn on fire in the hopes of killing all the "Devil Spiders."

After the fire finished consuming the barn, the family went to town to report what they had discovered. Many in town realized that they had been losing livestock for years and always thought it was coyotes or a thief.

They went to the remains of the burned barn and found an old private mine entrance in the basement. They followed it down, and still more webs were everywhere. Within they found a giant spider as big as the mine tunnel blocking further access. Again, killing the creature with fire seemed to be the only solution.

The curious after effect of this story is that families in the area will never let a barn fall into disrepair, unlike many other barns in other parts of the state.

THE JERSEY DEVIL

Pine Barrens, New Jersey

The epitome of the holler tale gone viral is that of the Jersey Devil. This story has so many variations in the nearly 250 years since it originated. While many do not associate New Jersey with the Appalachian heritage and folklore tales, this legend firmly fits the mold of most mountain monster lore.

The area this creature comes from is in southeastern New Jersey, a large dense conglomeration of swamp marsh and dense cedar forest. The area was very difficult to traverse, and Native American trails were sometimes the only paths available through these great obstacles of nature. This area is known as the Pine Barrens, a name that has existed since before the Revolutionary War.

The most famous account of the birth of this legend is that on a dark and stormy night in 1735, a Quaker gave birth to a child during a great thunderstorm. Many believed her to be a witch or, at the very least, enchanted. The woman was known as Mother Leeds, and she had many children already. When this child was born deformed, she cursed it, as it would put her into further debt. Another account claims that the child became more and more deformed as it grew older.

Mother Leeds locked the child up to hide her shame. The child grew stranger every day as it turned into a monster or demon. It had a horse's head and an elongated body. Wings sprouted from its shoulders. Its feet turned into cloven hooves. It finally grew a thick tail. The creature escaped up the chimney one night, and the rest is history.

There are other variations of this story involving a tryst between a British soldier and a young girl. Their child was cursed to become the Jersey Devil due to her act of treason against the Americans. Another claims that a young woman crossed a Romani and was cursed to bear the demonic child. A final version says that a man made a monstrous face mask to entertain children, but it became so popular that he never removed it. None of these tales is repeated as much as the Mother Leeds version. Early accounts even refer to the creature as the "Leeds Devil."

As he is a "Devil," his reputation expanded. If your crops failed, it was due to the Jersey Devil. Cows fail to give good milk? "The Jersey Devil has struck again." Any livestock gone missing? "Had to be the Jersey Devil!" Stories became that he returned every seven years like locusts. He would be an omen of war, drought and other unspeakable disasters.

The Jersey Devil has become a pop culture sensation that started from a simple folktale.
Illustration by Kari Schultz.

There were sightings reported all over the area. Many included noted witnesses like police officers, postal workers and local businesspeople. His tracks were often seen in the snow of winter.

Famously, a naval hero of America, Commodore Stephen Decatur, spotted the creature and fired a cannonball right at it, but it did not even stagger the creature as it flew overhead. Even Napoleon's brother once took a shot at it while he was hunting in Bordentown, New Jersey.

The Devil has appeared all over New England, sticking to the woods and Appalachian foothills. He has been spotted in New York, Maryland, Pennsylvania and Delaware. In 1909, there was a one-week period where more than thirty sightings were reported in the papers of the area.

The Smithsonian Institute weighed in on the legend and claimed that it might have been some prehistoric creature that had lived in the limestone caves nearby. An extinct fissiped, some unique marsupial carnivore, a pterodactyl or the Thunderbird were all postulated in the papers by various scientific communities. Even the Mothman theory of an unusual sandhill crane migration was brought up.

The Jersey Devil sometimes has sometimes been attributed to benevolent stories. He has helped stranded travelers in the Pine Barrens by guiding them to safety. He became famous in the 1970s when the movie *The Legend of Boggy Hollow* brought his story to national attention.

In 1929, the Jersey Devil was declared the Official State Demon of New Jersey. This is a title only held by this creature. The twice governor of New Jersey Walter Edge was quoted, "When I was a boy…I was never threatened with the bogey man….We were threatened with the Jersey Devil, morning noon, and night."

The Jersey Devil is not going anywhere anytime soon. Sightings continue to this day. Would-be monster hunters seek him out as much as Bigfoot, Nessie or any other monster—even if it is only a famous holler legend.

THE BOGEY MEN

Olympia, Kentucky

In the small community around Olympia, Kentucky, there is a legend that goes back to when the town was just starting out. The local iron mine was just starting to turn a solid profit for the owners. Through some blasting, the miners broke through a wall and discovered an open cave.

When the wall came down, several of the miners were shaken by what they saw and refused to go back into the mine. They claimed to have seen a group of large and squat "toad-skinned" men that were eating what appeared to be the carcass of a bear. They had long claws and walked like bent-over hunchbacks, according to their account. The creatures had seemed undisturbed by the breaking of the wall.

One of the miners returned home immediately and wrote of the encounter with the strange "Bogey" people to his brother in the nearby city of Sharpsburg. He was asking his brother whether he should continue working in the haunted mine or not. His brother encouraged him to see what the mine owners would do about the Bogeys.

As the men refused to return to the mine, one of the owners put out an advertisement for game hunters to clear the mine of bears and other pests. Several trappers showed up to form a hunting party and went into the mine and the newly opened cave. The miner once again wrote to his brother of this development.

The miner stated that a short while after the men went into the entrance, they heard lots of gunfire echoing from the mines. One of the older miners

When the wall came down, the miners saw several strange "Bogey Men," who barely seemed to care that they were there. *Illustration by Kari Schultz.*

said that it reminded him of a Civil War battle he had been in. The hunting party came out with several bodies.

The miners were pleased to see that there were some of the Bogeys as well as a few bears among the dead. None of the hunters said a thing as they collected their bounty and went off back to parts unknown.

The miners returned to the dig, and the mine was worked for many years. No one ever mentioned the strange Bogeys. We only know of them at all from the letters between the brothers.

Then, on a cold December morning in 1885, the mine was about to dig deeper in the hopes of a new iron vein. The blasting dynamite charge was set, and the fuse was lit. After retiring to a safe distance, the miners waited a long while for the inevitable explosion. None came.

Figuring that the fuse was bad, the men went to replace it with a good one. Upon arrival, the blast went off. At least five men died in the explosion. The newspaper account of the explosion never confirmed the final tally, as most were day laborers. One man was said to have been blown twenty-five feet into the air and had his eyes blown out with iron ore debris.

The mine was closed for some time, and many said that it was cursed from killing the Bogey creatures ten years earlier. In the area today, the Rose Run iron tract is on private property. Visitors are not welcome without notice.

There are no further sightings of the Bogey men from the late 1800s. The explosion in 1885 appears to have been nothing more than a tragic accident. Appalachian folklore, though, likes to combine the two.

The Pope Lick Monster

Louisville, Kentucky

Pope Lick Park officially opened in 2013. It was formerly known as Floyd's Fork Park. It comprises centuries-old forest known as the Big Beech Woods and a nice grassland area. The Pope Lick Creek meanders through the park and the John Floyd Fields. There are plenty of nice hiking trails, and it is a lovely area just outside bustling Louisville. There is a lot of history here as well as a legendary beast.

John Floyd, for whom the park was originally named, was a colonel in the Kentucky Militia in the Revolutionary War. He went on several notable raids on British forces with Revolutionary War hero George Rogers Clark. Clark was known as the "Conqueror of the Old Northwest" due to his Illinois

Pope Lick Bridge is an active train trestle and should never be trespassed on. *Photo by the author.*

campaign that severely weakened British control of the Northwest Territory. Both men were noted during the signing of the 1783 Treaty of Paris.

Floyd held various careers through his life. He started on the family farm, but as soon as he was able, he moved to Virginia and became a teacher while living in the home of Colonel William Preston. Floyd and Preston turned to surveying land. Veterans of the French and Indian War had many claims to land in the area, including George Washington and Patrick Henry. They followed the Ohio and Kanawha Rivers for most of the trip.

Once entering what was called Kentucky County in 1774, they encountered some Shawnees who warned the expedition away. They had passes from the commandant at Fort Pitt. This was to sway white men from the area, as they held claim. It made the Ohio River the declared border of the Native American lands.

The surveyors continued their campaign and ignored the warning. Floyd found an area of two thousand acres that he would lay claim to and sent to be purchased. It lies in what is now St. Matthews, Kentucky. Floyd's party was attacked shortly thereafter, and two of his party were killed. His group fled south down the Ohio and onto the Mississippi River and finally down to New Orleans.

Floyd, however, fled west to Virginia and traversed it alone. He came across a group of locals rallying for the first stage of what would become Lord Dunmore's War. He met with Captain William Russel and noted frontiersmen Daniel Boone and Michael Stoner. Floyd went to form his own militia, feeling the need for revenge. His men followed the trail of the main army and arrived at the battle site that ended Dunmore's War in Point Pleasant just a day too late to participate.

Floyd and Boone helped found several camps along the Dix River and established the Transylvania Colony. This was the earliest form of government in the Allegheny Mountain area off the Appalachians. Floyd would later assist in the rescue of Jemima Boone from a Shawnee and Cherokee raiding party in 1776. That event would become a story told for generations in the area.

Floyd would later become a privateer and a marshal, and then he returned home to his parcel of land in Kentucky to settle. He built a temporary home for his family in what would now be the corner of Third and Main in Louisville. He was made the county lieutenant of Jefferson County in 1781. He led many campaigns against the Native American tribes of the area. He would later be named one of the first judges of Kentucky. He was killed by Native American warriors in 1783.

The river that flows through the park is named Floyds Fork, and the spot where it meets Salt River is where he had a disastrous campaign against a Shawnee tribe. This battle became widely known as Floyd's Folly or Floyd's Defeat.

Years passed, and Louisville grew into one of the largest cities in Kentucky. The area near Floyd's Folly became known as Fisherville. As the railroad came to town in the 1800s, a large trestle bridge was built over the fork. The Norfolk Southern Railroad is 90 feet high and goes across the span of 772 feet.

There are several stories starting around the 1940s of a strange goat man sighted in the area. He is often seen leaping off the bridge onto poor folks walking or riding under the trestle along the fork. What really sets this "Goat-man" legend apart from other horned beast stories in the Appalachian Mountains, like the Sheepsquatch, is that this creature carries a tribal tomahawk. In later versions of the legend, it wields the axe of a modern woodsman.

Tales of the creature say that he was summoned by a farmer seeking power and using dark magic. One other tale says that it was summoned by the natives after the stealing of the land and that it seeks vengeance for the wrongs done to their people.

The most common telling of the legend is that Pope Lick Monster was a creature captured in the wilds of Canada that became the star attraction of a traveling circus freak show. He has the legs and hooves of a goat with the torso of an alabaster-skinned man. He has a human-shaped face with

The infamous Pope Lick Monster. *Illustration by Kari Schultz.*

eyes set wide apart. He also has the horns of a great ram. While touring, the circus train derailed over the bridge, and the creature escaped into the nearby hills.

The creature has been described as having several powers to lure people out onto the bridge. The monster is said to lure people onto the bridge with hypnosis. Sometimes it uses voice mimicry to pretend to be a friend or family member and calls to you to come help them on the bridge. Then they face the monster or an oncoming train.

There is no history of the legend prior to the 1940s. Numerous deaths are sadly associated with the bridge. From suicides to legend trippers falling to their death, there are no greater legends with a higher true death toll. Most recently in May 2019, Savanah Bright, a young fifteen-year-old girl, was found dead at the bottom of the bridge. Her young friend survived and said that they were out looking for the monster.

There have been at least four confirmed deaths of people climbing on the bridge looking for the monster. Most thought the bridge to be abandoned. In truth, the track is frequently used, at least several times a day. The bridge is off limits and fenced off, but people still trespass.

If you go to visit Pope Lick, feel free to visit from the ground underneath. There is a nice park with parking a short distance away with a scenic trail along the river. As you pass under the bridge, pay your respects at the markers for Savannah and others. If you want to explore the bridge from above, that is what drones are for. Stay safe.

THE RAT MAN

Jackson, Kentucky

In a small holler near Jackson, Kentucky, there is a peculiar pile of rocks built like a shrine at the foot of a nearby hill. The pile of rocks has offerings left on it in the form of empty bottles of beer and sodas, half-smoked cigarettes and hundreds upon hundreds of bottle caps. In each bottle is a note requesting a favor from the Rat Man.

The story is told that the Rat Man started as a trapper and woodsman in the area around the time of the early European settlers. He would help those in the area get familiar with the woods and the local flora and fauna. He also acted as a go-between for the local native tribes and the new settlers.

One day, he decided that he wanted to marry the local priest's daughter, whom he had been courting. The family wanted nothing to do with this "man of the woods" and refused to allow the marriage. They married her off to a young "proper" man in a nearby town and sent her away. The wild man met with the local tribe of Native Americans and had their shaman curse the valley.

From then on, the people of the valley had to leave presents for the Rat Man or he would take their animals, cause crops to fail or create other general unpleasantness to befall the nearby farms. The Rat Man is seen to this day coming to the offering place. He wears tattered robes and collects the bottles and caps once every blue moon.

Varying versions of this legend tell that the Rat Man is the old trapper, who turned into this legendary beast. Other versions say that it is the priest who was cursed, and he was turned into the creature himself. A final version says it is the illegitimate child of the trapper and the priest's daughter who was cursed to be the beastly creature.

Why he grants wishes and boons for treats is never really explained in any of the stories. There was a story that the city hall once had a small shrine in the alley behind it in the 1970s, but we could find no proof of that or even an alley.

The family who shared this with us said that the shrine has moved farther back from the road, so you have to really look for it now. They say that once every few months, they leave an offering of bottle caps and other trinkets for the Rat Man, just to be safe.

THE WHITE THANGS

Various, Alabama and West Virginia

The White Thangs of the hills are well known throughout various hollers all across the Appalachian Mountains. They are not to be confused with the White Thang of Pennsylvania, which is an albino Bigfoot and detailed in that latter section of this book.

These creatures are shapeshifting animals that are sometimes described as looking like exceptionally large wolves or dogs. Some stories describe them as being able to make themselves look like lions, bears or even horse-sized badgers. In whatever form they appear, they are always covered in long fur that is snowy white. Usually, they have oversized mouths full of razor-sharp fangs.

Occasionally they will be detailed as having too many legs for whatever animal they resemble. They are known to run at incredible speeds. They have a cry that sounds like a wailing woman. They have been known to charge at witnesses but seem to disappear as everyone closes their eyes and prepares to be slain by the ravenous beasts. That is not to say they are harmless, as like other stories of these legendary beasts, livestock and pets are their favorite targets. Many of the animals that are attacked by the White Thangs are left mutilated, with no traces of blood.

In the ways of the Cherokees, the appearance of a white wolf signaled death. In the Appalachian version, the wolf has become a dog. The large white dog will appear and follow you home. It is there to let you know you will be visited by death soon with the loss of someone close to you. Some claim that the dog can only be seen by the one who first spotted it.

White Thangs are often associated with cemeteries as guardian spirits. This could tie to the Cherokee lore. They are frequently described as being solid, though, and not spectral or intangible. They are very real to those who see them.

THE SNALLYGASTER

South Mountain, Maryland

The Snallygaster grew to fame in Frederick County, Maryland. The creature is a strange hybrid that seems to be part bird and part dragon and perhaps even has some metallic parts. This giant creature nests in caves and flies silently in the skies. It can swoop down on unsuspecting prey, including children.

The strange name of the beast comes from German immigrants to the area. They called the creature the Schneller Geist. This translates as "quick spirit" in English. All the early tales from the 1700s describe the creature as being a bird with demonic features. Some variations on the tale claim that the beast had tentacles coming out of its mouth that could drain the blood from its victims.

The Snallygaster was little more than a folktale until 1909, when Maryland newspapers began to run stories about its appearance. Between February and March, there were dozens of stories printed with frequent sightings of the creature. It was described as having a long-pointed bill, claws made of steel and a giant eye in the middle of its head.

One article claimed that a grown man was carried aloft by the creature, which killed him by draining his blood. It then dropped the body on a nearby hillside as it flew away. Hunters taking shots at the creature remarked that although they hit the beast, they could not tell if it was hurt at all.

The Smithsonian Institute offered a reward for the creature. Then President Theodore Roosevelt considered postponing an important

What is the Snallygaster? Its description defies explanation. *Illustration by Kari Schultz.*

international diplomatic trip. He wanted to go hunt the strange creature personally.

Although primarily associated with the Northeast, the creature traveled all throughout the Appalachians and even beyond. Newspaper accounts seemed to pop up everywhere. A woman claimed that she was almost abducted by the creature herself near the town of Scrabble, West Virginia. In nearby Sharpsburg, a farmer claimed that the beast had been roosting in his barn on a giant egg.

It was seen again in Ohio a few times before seeming to return to Maryland again. Several of the sightings claimed that it had laid eggs. Others were tales of it flying overhead and screeching like an enormous hawk.

The beast disappeared into legend until about twenty years later, when sightings skyrocketed again. Many were from the same areas of the original sightings. This led many to believe that this next round of sightings represented the offspring of the original creature. Perhaps a twenty-year gestation was not uncommon for such a large and unusual beast.

The last reported sighting involved one that fell into a moonshine vat. The vat and creature were destroyed by government agents during Prohibition. Sadly, no records of this event other than a story in a lone newspaper in Pennsylvania exist to verify the account.

THE SNARLY YOW

Harpers Ferry, West Virginia

A large, ghostly black dog was frequently seen along the road from South Mountain, Maryland, to Harpers Ferry, West Virginia. The creature had a vast territory and was seen often enough that the area called him the Snarly Yow. This was again from German immigrants, who had named it for the fearsome growl it would make.

Many stories would claim that the creature could change size and shape. Generally, it was a large black dog that dragged a chain behind it. Sometimes in the full moonlight it would change to a pale white coat. The stories say that if it went with its white coat, sometimes the head would disappear completely as well.

An inn along the road knew of the creature well. It would warn travelers that the Snarly Yow would spook their horses and to be extra careful when riding out in the early mornings. The stories date back to some written accounts as early as 1790.

In 1882, the Snarly Yow was documented in a book called *South Mountain Magic* by Madeline Dahlgren. It is required reading for those wanting to know more of the monsters and legends of the pre-1900s northeastern United States. The book chronicles several sightings of the Snarly Yow.

One encounter tells of a road-weary traveler who encountered a large black dog across the road from him. The creature began to grow in size and open its immense jaws. The man jumped onto his horse to flee. The dog let out a wail that spooked his horse so badly that it kicked him in the head. He barely escaped with his life.

There is a plaque on the road near Boonsboro, Maryland, for the Battle of South Mountain in the Civil War. On the display is a sidebar note, which reads as follows: "Beware of the 'Snarly Yow.' Legend has it that the shadow of a black dog used to prowl the heights of South Mountain. One night, a huntsman, famous as a sure shot, encountered the beast. He aimed and fired his rifle. The shot went right through the animal with no effect. He fired again and again, each shot passing through the shadowy beast. Finally overcome with dread, the huntsman fled."

The Snarly Yow is seen often even in modern times. It has an affinity for chasing cars, just like normal dogs. Some fear that they may have hit a dog on the road, as it runs out in front of their vehicle. The drivers are shocked to discover the creature unharmed and baring its fangs at them before vanishing into thin air.

THE WAMPUS CAT

Appalachian Mountain Legend, Various States

Another frequently told and widely known creature is the Wampus Cat. In Native American culture, it is a benevolent beast that protects sacred lands. In some stories, it is a magical creature that can stare at you so hard it will drive you to madness. Some stories have connected it to the Underwater Panther as a fellow guardian of the earth and waters.

The Wampus Cat's appearance is as varied as the stories about it. Often it is half-cat and half-canine, with the head of a woman. Some say it changes color as the sun sets—dark fur when it is light and brighter colors in the night sky as it is often described. Many times it is seen walking on its hind legs.

There can be many signs of a Wampus Cat in your area. The cat's footprints are only visible on solid rock. Moonlight glinting off its eyes is said to start forest fires. If a Wampus Cat travels in your river or creek, the fish will not bite until the next full moon. The beast will steal mining tools and use them to sharpen its teeth and claws. The howl of a Wampus Cat can curdle the freshest milk.

Out of the Appalachians, the Wampus Cat has found a home in Idaho. That state claims it as its own and even has many schools with the Wampus Cat as a mascot. The stories there say that the Wampus Cat kills eagles, which early trappers were not fond of. The eagles would often claim the deer they would hunt. They thanked the Wampus Cat for culling the eagles.

The Cherokees are credited with the lore of the Wampus Cat. In some tales, the cat is known as Ewah. She was a Cherokee woman who did not trust her husband. She snuck out to follow him one evening and put on the skin of a mountain lion to hide. Mistakenly, she observed a sacred ritual. When discovered, the shaman of the tribe cursed her to wear the hide forever. This completely transformed the woman into the Wampus Cat.

An even more popular tale tells that Ewah was a demon that terrorized a Cherokee village. A great warrior was sent to fight the demon, but he was laid low by the beast. The warrior's wife claimed the right to slay Ewah. To protect herself, she had the shaman turn her into a bobcat to hide her scent and give her great agility. She surprised Ewah and defeated the beast. Her spirit, though, was trapped forever in the bobcat. Now she protects the tribes and all they hold sacred.

The Wampus Cat is sighted all throughout the Appalachians and is frequently blamed for livestock disappearances to this very day.

THE LIZARD MAN OF SCAPE ORE SWAMP

Bishopville, South Carolina

On the night of June 29, 1988, a young man named Christopher Davis was driving home along the road that crosses through Scape Ore Swamp just outside Bishopville, South Carolina. He had a blowout and had to pull to the shoulder to change his tire. After completing the change and putting the old tire in his trunk, something caught his attention in the swampy area beside him.

> *I looked back and saw something running across the field towards me. It was about 25 yards away and I saw red eyes glowing. I ran into the car and as I locked it, the thing grabbed the door handle. I could see him from the neck down—the three big fingers, long black nails and green rough skin. It was strong and angry.*
>
> *I looked in my mirror and saw a blur of green running. I could see his toes and then he jumped on the roof of my car. I thought I heard a grunt and then I could see his fingers through the front windshield, where they curled around on the roof. I sped up and swerved to shake the creature off.*

The sign at the Harry & Harry Too. It lies just outside the Scape Ore Swamp. The diner in this converted old house celebrates all things Lizard Man. *Photo by the author.*

Once he returned to his home, he told his parents, who then called the police. The local sheriff of Lee County at the time was Liston Truesdale. The sheriff took the report and noted the damage on the car, notably the scratches on the roof of the car. The evidence reinforced the boy's story. Unbeknownst to Davis, there had been other reports in the area with similar signs of damage.

Davis agreed to take a polygraph test. He passed it, and it was determined that there would be further investigation into the strange encounter. The Lee County Police Department would be on the lookout for more odd cases. It did not have to wait long.

A few weeks later in mid-July, the Wayne family made a report that their car had been damaged by some animal. The sidewalls had been dented and scratched. The hood ornament had been broken. The antenna for the radio had been bent. Wires were pulled. The molding had been chewed. There were strange muddy footprints all over the vehicle. Deputies investigated the area and even went back to Scape Ore Swamp. There they found three-toed tracks of unusual size and made plaster casts.

Another few weeks passed and a man claimed to have seen the creature and shot it just outside nearby Shaw Air Force Base. He claimed to have wounded the creature, possibly mortally. He later took back this report as he was about to be charged with the illegal ownership of a handgun. He was then charged with filing a false police report.

Over the next few months, the number of sightings increased. Families from multiple states all claimed to have seen the creature for generations migrate along the rivers of the Appalachian Mountains that would eventually lead down to Scape Ore Swamp. The descriptions were always of a humanlike creature with green or gray scales and bright-red eyes. It was always at least seven feet tall and built like football linebacker.

MCOS, a local radio station, offered a reward of $1 million for the capture of the Beast of Bishopville. The number of reports exploded with the reward offer, but they were less and less credible every call. With the boom of tourists and would-be monster hunters to the area, the police felt that it was only a matter of time before someone got hurt.

The bubble burst when one of the residents of the airbase was caught putting on a lizard suit. The furor died down, as clearly it was all just a hoax. Locals still see the creature and insist that it is real, though. In 2005, there was a sighting of a pair of the creatures in nearby Newberry, South Carolina. These creatures had the green skin and glowing red eyes so often associated with the older sightings. The woman who reported them claimed to have never heard of the creature and thought they might be hairless sasquatches.

The creature has not been limited to South Carolina. There are stories of Lizard folk all along the Appalachian rivers and creeks. Some stories of the Shawnees claim to have had great battles with the reptile men tribes over a sacred spring near what is now Cherokee, Tennessee.

The people in Bishopville love their local monster. There is a semi-annual Lizard Man Festival that was started in 2018 but has not reoccurred as of yet. There are several places in town that celebrate the creature. A must visit is the Harry & Harry Too, which has a great Lizard Man theme with some great local delicacies. The shrimp and grits there are a must.

In August 2017, just before the solar eclipse, the South Carolina Emergency Management System sent a tweet saying that the residents of Lee and Sumter County should "remain vigilant" during the eclipse. It was not certain how the eclipse might affect the Lizard Man population in the area.

There were no sightings during the eclipse…none that was reported at any rate.

BUNNY MAN BRIDGE

Clifton, Virginia

The tale goes that if you approach the strange tunnel just outside the town of Clifton, Virginia, on Halloween night, you will be visited by a man dressed in a bunny suit. This odd man will attack you with his axe and chop you into

The Bunny Man, with his axe, stands outside Bunny Man Bridge. *Illustration by Kari Schultz.*

pieces. He will decorate the trees around the tunnel with your remains for all to see, and all will fear the return of the Bunny Man.

Another version of the legend says that all you have to do is say his name three times near the old tunnel and the Bunny Man will come and get you.

In still another tale, he is the ghost of an escaped mental patient. He ate rabbits and wears their skins. His wife and child were murdered. He was the primary suspect due to his odd behavior, but he was acquitted. The town did not believe his innocence. They tortured him with accusations and slander and drove him mad. One Halloween, he had enough and mutilated some of the town's children in retaliation.

The one-lane tunnel on Colchester Road has so many legends. Many travel to legend-trip this site, as it is not difficult to access. The police have to patrol the area on Halloween, as it gets far too crowded with folks looking for that ultimate scare. This holler legend went viral quickly in the modern internet age.

The nearby haunted attraction of the Clifton Haunted Trail features the Bunny Man prominently in its advertising. Thousands flock to its event every Halloween.

Fairfax Library's resident archivist, Brian Conley, has done more research on the Bunny Man legend than anyone alive. He has been researching possible origins of the story most of his life. He drafted the definitive paper on the subject in 2008 called "The Bunny Man Unmasked: The Real Life Origins of an Urban Legend." In his paper, he detailed several older historical events that might have combined into this one amalgamation of an urban legend.

In February 1949, a mother and her baby were slain and buried in a shallow grave just outside the nearby town of Fairfax. The husband was convicted of their murders and sent to Pennhurst Mental Institution.

Another piece of the legend fell into place when an article was found from October 22, 1970. In this a man in a bunny suit was sought after for throwing an axe through the window of an air force cadet who was parking with his girlfriend in Fairfax.

The Bunny Man was seen again just a week later in Fairfax. This time, he was chopping at a house under construction with his axe. When confronted, the man in the suit with floppy ears skipped away before he could be apprehended. After a few weeks, the case was filed away as unsolved. No one was ever caught.

So, there is some truth to the legend in several events, but nothing ties it directly to the tunnel itself. The name Bunny Man Bridge is also a misnomer, as it is a tunnel and not a bridge at all. Conley is happy to share his knowledge of the legend with visitors to the library.

OL' PETE

Rutledge, Tennessee

Just a short drive from the tourist havens of the Smoky Mountains in Pigeon Forge and Gatlinburg lies a small community just outside the town of Rutledge, Tennessee. The mountains in this area were sparsely inhabited for a very long time. Only recently, with the booming of the nearby tourist areas, has modern life broken into these hollers.

There is one man here who still lives by an old code. No one seemed to know his name. They all knew his large dog though: Ol' Pete. The dog was a mean-spirited creature that looked like a cross between a bloodhound and pit bull and was as big as a pack mule. Everyone talks in hushed tones about the bald man and Ol' Pete.

According to those who live there, the man had been there as long as anyone could remember. There are stories that he made a deal with the Cherokees to protect the valley's game and wildlife from the incoming European settlers in exchange for the power to grant wishes.

His power came with a price. His dog became possessed by the spirit of a manitou. This creature would have the power to grant the wishes sought. The greater the wish, the more significant the cost. Ol' Pete and the evil spirit within him would consume the offering made for the boon.

If the offering was not significant enough to appease the hound, it was known to take a limb off your very body. The price could be easy for a simple boon. Need a small loan of money? Then a family heirloom would suffice. Need the life of a loved one spared from illness? That would cost you the family pet's life.

The stories go that someone once wanted to protect their entire family from a rival clan in a blood feud. Ol' Pete was said to have granted the wish, but only after consuming all of the youngest children in the family.

Ol' Pete is the demonic hound of a mysterious stranger. He could grant you a favor, but "Beware the Dog!" *Illustration by Kari Schultz.*

One person was said to have been granted their wish but tried to renege on their offering by giving up a neighbor's prized raccoon hunting dog. Ol' Pete was not easily fooled. He refused the offer. The old man held the one that had tried to fool them as the hound cleanly ate both of his legs. The wish had apparently been for fine work boots. Ol' Pete and the bald man made certain that he would have no need for boots again.

Neither Ol' Pete nor his handler have been seen for decades. The family who speaks of him says that he may have passed in the 1960s, but the stories say that he would have been nearly two hundred years old. That's a long time for a man to live. It's even longer in dog years for the hellhound Ol' Pete.

THE MAN AT THE CROSSROADS

Harlan, Kentucky

Deals with the devil himself go back to Faust in 1587, when he was summoned at a crossroads. The folklore of this predates that by a number of years. The stories go that most any crossroads can be used to summon a devil or demon if one knows the right call. Blues sensation Robert Johnson claimed to have gained his talents by doing that very thing in the 1930s.

Just outside Harlan, Kentucky, however, there is a crossroad that a devil visits a little more often. The devil here may not be Satan himself, but he is no less a threat. He is spoken about in hushed whispers, and the town church is barred at night to keep him at bay.

Temptation is a formidable force though. The Harlan Crossroads Devil always seems to know when he is wanted. There are many stories of the devil there, with his kind face and gracious smile, comforting those in grief. He spurs them to acts of aggression against those who have wronged them. He is known to turn jealous lovers into coldblooded killers.

Harlan is no stranger to tragedy. Some of the worst coal mining disasters in the world have occurred in the past near here. These tragic accidents were sometimes blamed on the actions of the "Man at the Crossroads." Still others say that the accidents happen so that people will come to him for solace.

In 1975, a woman visited the Harlan crossroads in the hopes of finding the man. He was already sitting on a tree stump just across from her as she arrived. She said he was well dressed and had very dark hair. The man already knew that she wanted a child. She had lost her eldest son in a mining accident the year before.

The suited man told her to go home and that night she and her husband would make a new baby. When she returned home with the good news, she told her husband. He was so sad that she had turned to the devil instead of God; he asked her what would her lost child think.

They wept and prayed together for the evening. She returned to the crossroads the next day. There the man in the suit still sat on his stump. He approached her and asked if they had made the child the previous night. She told him no—that they had prayed and would not be having any more children.

The man at the crossroads got his child soon anyway. The woman's eldest daughter had a tryst with a handsome stranger from town that night. She was with child, and it was to be born out of wedlock. The family

What could he offer you to make a deal with a demon at a crossroads at midnight? *Illustration by Kari Schultz.*

was highly embarrassed at the time. When the young girl told her mother of the baby's father, she realized it was the devil himself.

After the daughter gave birth to her child, both were sent away immediately to live with distant relatives in another state. No one really knows what happened to them. The child was claimed to have a small tail and cloven feet. Perhaps they went to New Jersey to meet with the Leeds Devil?

IT BITES

Evington, Virginia

Just outside the historic town of Evington, Virginia, there is a small cluster of old farms just off U.S. Highway 29. One family there was particularly good at making moonshine during Prohibition. They would supply their illegal alcohol to many areas around the state. The farms all worked together to protect the operation from outsiders.

Any shadow could contain this creature. Be careful! It bites! *Illustration by Kari Schultz*.

As larger illegal operations moved into the state, particularly on the East Coast in more urban areas some miles away, the business of 'shine running was beginning to be more trouble than it was worth. A particularly studious member of the family decided that he could make a better moonshine if he added in some his old family medicinal recipes.

What he did not know was that those recipes were from his grandmother's European book of old magic spells and hexes. The roots they added to the 'shine were of a mystical nature, and mixed with the highly potent alcohol, they were incredibly powerful. The first round of testing went well, and the "shiners" had a great party with all the local farms to celebrate their new brew.

It was during the party that the budding young chemist noticed a constant sense of movement out of the corners of his eyes. Something was hurrying from shadow to shadow. He immediately thought that rats might be getting into their crops in storage and roused other partygoers to the threat to their stores. Weapons were drawn.

People began to shriek and scream as they, too, began to see the darting movements in the shadows. Gunshots began to ring out as people began to blast the small dark intruders. It did not take long for many to realize that it was not rats.

The strange creatures in the shadows seemed to be slick and oily. They were small black balls of wet dripping teeth. Light seemed to not be able to catch them as they moved quickly from shadow to shadow. Fires began to be lit wherever there was a dark spot in hopes of driving away the strange creatures.

One brave soul thought that he had cornered one and tried to catch it in an empty feed sack. The creature moved like lightning and nearly severed his hand at the wrist. He screamed, "It bites! It bites!"

By the next morning, everyone had calmed down and agreed that it must simply have been the 'shine causing everyone to make a fuss. There were several wounded people, and the 'shine ring got busted when the police arrived to investigate the aftermath.

The budding chemist was forever changed. He wound up in a nearby asylum. He was convinced that the creatures were not hallucinations or alcoholic-induced nightmares. He was convinced that they exist in every shadow and that the strange, exotic mixture had opened the mind's eye to be able to see them. He now lived in mortal fear of the dark. He would scream every night when the lights would be turned off, "It bites!"

PART V
THE SASQUATCH ENCOUNTERS

BIGFOOT IN THE APPALACHIANS

The forests of the Appalachians extend from Quebec to Alabama. Sometimes they spread beyond the mountains themselves into the nearby flatlands that outskirt the oldest mountain range in the world. The forests along the Appalachian Trail are considered by many researchers to be the main transport route used by Sasquatch for migration up and down the East Coast. This area would be the perfect place for them to hide well out of the way of modern humans.

The Appalachian plateau—which covers parts of Pennsylvania, Kentucky, West Virginia and eastern Ohio—is on the western edge of the mountain range. Sasquatch has been documented in these forests for as long as anyone can remember. While not as famous as the Pacific Northwest sightings, the incidents here are no less numerous.

The largest state park in Ohio is Salt Fork Park. This area is well known among Bigfoot hunters. With well over seventeen thousand acres of forest and plenty of rivers, lakes, and streams, this would seem to be the perfect place for a colony of large undiscovered creatures to call home.

The Appalachians are well known for Bigfoot sightings. Some are just a few miles outside well-populated cities. Skeptics often claim that there should be more sightings than there are. If the numbers of reports keep increasing as they have in recent years, this argument is proving its own point. Sasquatch reporting organizations have consistently seen drastic rises in recent sightings.

Some of the exhibits at Expedition Bigfoot in Blue Ridge, Georgia. *Photo by the author.*

Skeptics also say that there simply is not enough food for such a population of large ape like creatures to exist in the mountains. Researchers disagree, noting that if the creature hunts, there is plenty of game to be had. They might even be able to go prolonged periods without eating, like bears. If they are herbivores or omnivores, there are certainly plenty of options available for large caloric intake in the woods along the Appalachians.

The Bigfoot Research Geographical Database shows that the Appalachian Plateau is high up on the concentration of sightings. Its numbers are right on par with the northwestern United States and Florida. Eastern Ohio seems to be the current hot spot.

Like any wild animal, Sasquatch must require food, shelter and safety. They would find this easily throughout the Appalachians. There have been sightings in every mountain state, most notably in Pennsylvania, Virginia, West Virginia, Kentucky, Tennessee, Georgia, New Jersey and even rural New York. The big question is: How has it dodged hunters for so long?

Most researchers agree that they are very smart, very adapted to hide with their amazing natural camouflage, and they stay away from populated areas. Like the recent sightings of big cats, long thought near extinction in the Appalachians, the hope remains for that perfect bit of evidence to prove the existence of Bigfoot to the world.

There are stories of encounters that have become legends in their own right.

THE OHIO GRASSMAN

Eastern Ohio

In 1869, the first sightings began of a large, hairy creature that stood nine feet tall, reported in the woods of Eastern Ohio and Western Pennsylvania. For more than 150 years, the reports of this creature, called the Grassman, have endured. He is known to roam rural fields and terrorize farms and livestock.

Notably, the creature was documented eating tall grasses, which gave it its name. It is believed by researchers that this particular Bigfoot colony might have adapted its diet, as the areas were prone to producing cereal crops. These would form a much easier source of food for hungry animals in the area if they were more omnivorous.

While similar to other Bigfoot sightings, the Grassmen tends to be much more communal. Frequently they are sighted in groups or pairs, unlike the typically solitary Bigfoot sightings. Like the Skunk Ape of Florida, the Grassman is also said to give off an extraordinarily strong foul odor to those near enough.

Many researchers point to the history of the region as being particularly receptive to a Sasquatch population. Ohio in 1800 only had a grand total of thirty-four thousand European settlers. To put this in perspective, New York City had more than fifty thousand people alone at this time. The Native American populations in Ohio were nearly gone at this time as well. By the 1600s, a combination of disease and war with the Iroquois tribes had greatly diminished the few tribes of the area. They would recover in time, but not to any great extent.

This means that while the lands east of the Appalachians were very prosperous and growing, most of this area comprised scattered settlements and farms. The Native American tribes were fleeing west to avoid the European settlers. The Ohio Proclamation Line of 1763 also helped to limit colonial expansion for some time.

All of this would have delayed the population boom to the Appalachians and beyond, allowing for Sasquatch to adapt to the coming of the large numbers

The Ohio Grassman is similar to most other detailed Sasquatch encounters. He stands about seven to eight feet tall but was known to have "rock star hair." *Illustration by Kari Schultz.*

of people who would encroach on its territory. The cougars and black bears, sadly, did not have these historical buffers to protect them as well.

The Ohio Grassman is seen quite often in Eastern Ohio. Despite the state now housing several million residents, there are still large areas of rural farms and dense forests with little human interaction. Sightings are reported to the Bigfoot Field Researchers Organization nearly weekly.

In 2016, a hunter and his son, Bill and Jimmy Conner, were returning to their truck from a day of hunting pheasant. As they exited the woods, they noted how suddenly quiet the area became. No animals were making any noise. Even the insects had suddenly become silent. They noted the eerie sensation of being watched.

A strong odor was suddenly upon them, and Jimmy, the son, admitted to thinking something terrible must have just happened nearby. He said it reminded him of a time the family had butchered a sick hog on their farm, and the smell had made him wretch. This was at least as foul a smell, and he felt nauseous.

Bill went to unsling his rifle but stopped short when he saw a large hairy creature stand up in the nearby field. He saw it was heading to the woods on the far side of the field. By looking at the trees, he estimated the creature to be at least eight feet tall and extremely broad-shouldered.

Jimmy broke the silence, "Dad, is that the Grassman?"

The creature turned immediately toward them and let out a strange howl that they claimed seemed to reverberate through the hills. The creature then sped off into the trees very quickly. The hunters gathered up their courage and went after it but could find no trace of it in the far woods. It had appeared to vanish into thin air. Noticeably, they said it looked like the Bigfoot with "rock star hair."

The family told a friend, who got them to report the incident to the BFRO. The organization sent a team to the area and found several sets of tracks that it was able to make casts of. It also noted unusual tree structures that seemed like makeshift shelters or dens.

Folks in Eastern Ohio have long known of the Grassman, and it looks like he is not going anywhere anytime soon.

The Minerva Monster

Minerva, Ohio

In 1978, the Clayton family reported to their local sheriff that they had encountered a hairy, seven-foot-tall monster just outside their home near Minerva, Ohio. The police came and investigated but found no evidence other than some odd footprints.

Their first sighting was in August, when Evelyn and Howe Clayton were spending time with their grandchildren. The kids ran inside screaming about the hairy monster they had seen in the nearby gravel pit. The couple went outside and immediately saw the creature the children had described.

The monster was squatting in the gravel pit and going through some refuse piled there. It was huge and covered with dark, matted fur. When it stood up, it was incredibly tall, and they estimated it had to be at least three hundred pounds of muscle.

The family fled back to their home to call the police. By the time they arrived, there were only footprints remaining. The Claytons noted that just days before the incident, the family's German Shepherd had been found dead with a broken neck in the gravel pit. They speculated that the beast must have done the foul deed.

The Minerva Monster, as it began to be called, would appear to the Claytons several more times. Once they saw the face of the beast peering into the home through the windows. On another occasion, they saw two of the creatures on a hill near the pit.

The newspapers and television stations of the time widely reported on the incident due to the police involvement with the case. It was also at the height of the popularity of *In Search of…*. Bigfoot mania was sweeping the world. The family was interviewed over and over for months.

The Minerva Monster was observed in broad daylight, which makes arguments of a misidentified animal in this case hard to argue. The family were very credible. Police involvement also leads to this being one of the most reliable accounts of a Bigfoot sighting on record. Some still contend that it was a very elaborate hoax.

Seth Breedlove of Small Town Monsters has made an incredible documentary on the Minerva Monster sighting, and it is highly recommended viewing for those interested in learning more about the encounter in 1978.

THE APPLE DEVILS

Marlinton, West Virginia

During the height of Mothman mania in the late 1960s, a lesser-known story was making the rounds of West Virginia in the southeastern part of the state. Reports began to appear of ape-like creatures with extremely long arms stripping some of the local apple orchards in the area of their fruit. Some big game hunters in the state looking for Mothman even came down to investigate the possibility of a group of escaped circus gorillas or monkeys in the area.

The creatures were notably shorter than most other Sasquatch sightings when described. Most were the same height as an average human or smaller. Some stories claimed that they were only five feet tall. The creatures got

The Apple Devils are very similar to other Sasquatch sightings but are noted for their very long arms and lean build. *Illustration by Kari Schultz.*

their name from stripping fruit trees with arms that seemed unusually long, almost as long as their height.

Dubbed the "Apple Devils" by the press, they were noted to be very quick when alerted to observers, often fleeing while running into the nearby forests of the area. They were very quiet and made no roars of grunts. One report did mention that one of the creatures made a soft *harrumph* sound when startled.

Again, these smaller Sasquatch were noted to have a distinct, sour smell to them. While not as strong as the Skunk Ape or Grassman, they were still unpleasant to be nearby. They tended to be of a reddish color or ruddy brown, according to witness statements.

The hunters who came discovered large nests in the branches of trees, which led some researchers into believing that these Sasquatch are more arboreal than their other cousins in the Appalachian area. They might even sleep in tree canopies. Again, they seemed to be more communal, with group sightings much more frequent than solo encounters.

Most skeptics agree that these are most likely a group of chimpanzees, apes or orangutans from a circus, zoo or carnival that had found easy fruit to pick. To the families in the area, these devils were not apes, but rather definitely a type of Bigfoot.

ORANGE EYES

Mill Lake, Ohio

Orange Eyes is often combined with the Ohio Grassman in sighting reports. He officially had his first sighting in 1963 near the wooded area of Mill Lake, Ohio. If there is a king or alpha of Sasquatch, then Orange Eyes might be it.

This Sasquatch is often described as being the largest creature any observer has ever seen. He has been estimated to be nearly eleven feet in height and must weigh nearly a ton. If reports are to be believed, this would make him one of the largest Bigfoot on record.

The initial sighting came from a young couple out for a walk when they stumbled on the creature. Once it stood to its full height and they had taken in the immensity of the beast, they fled back to their home. After calming down and describing the sheer size of the beast and its bright-orange eyes, a posse was formed among the townsfolk to hunt and kill this monster.

The armed mob found nothing. The locals postulated that it could be a peaceful creature, as the witness described nothing threatening in its behavior. Some felt it had only been driven out into more civilized areas due to recent construction of a nearby highway.

In April 1968, a second sighting was reported. A group of children claimed to have spotted the beast and chased it with baseball bats and a rope to attempt to catch the great beast. Amazingly, Orange Eyes evaded capture from these intrepid children. He then disappeared into legend for a long time. Legends seemed to dictate that he had retreated into the sewer systems of the growing population centers like Cleveland or Columbus.

Then, in 1991, two fishermen in Willis Creek saw the giant Bigfoot once again. They attempted to get to the car to get a camera. The beast fled when they splashed back to shore. They described him as being the largest ape they had ever seen. One of the fishermen remarked how it looked so different from what he thought it should have looked like, thanks to *The Six Million Dollar Man* episode with Bigfoot he had seen as a kid.

THE WHITE THANG

Blakeslee, Pennsylvania

There are several standout stories of Sasquatch that appear to be albino. Their fur is a bright white color. This is either a unique Bigfoot or as rare as albinos are among other species on the planet. They are not to be confused with other "White Thangs," which are usually shapeshifters in Alabama.

The White Thang of Pennsylvania was seen in 1970 near the town of Blakeslee. The witness was a young woman who saw a creature about seven feet tall with a long neck and broad chest. It was covered in a matted white fur. She described it as such: "Its eyes were dark and spaced far apart. Its white hair covered the lower half of its face. There was pinkish skin around the eyes and forehead. It looked like its hair was a little longer on its head and hanging over its forehead like bangs." The sighting was reported in local paper and attributed to Annette B. There are no more records of this sighting.

Just a few years later, in September 1973, two young girls were out late in a nearby area of the original sighting. They claimed to see a large creature covered in white fur with glowing red eyes. They claimed that it was carrying some sort of glowing white orb. They ran home and told their parents. The families went out to hunt the creature but found no sign of it.

The orb is an interesting twist to this sighting. It would be repeated in other sightings later in the same year. In the nearby town of Uniontown,

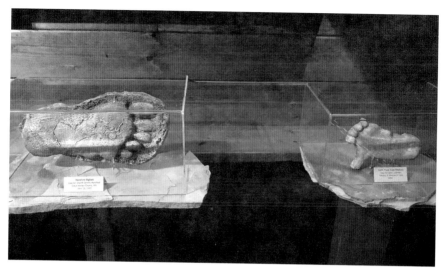

Expedition Bigfoot is a must stop in the mountains of North Georgia for Sasquatch enthusiasts. Here are some of the replicas of casts of famous Sasquatch prints. *Photo by the author.*

Pennsylvania, people claimed to see a glowing orb near two Bigfoot-like creatures that seemed to be jumping and thrashing around it.

The White Thang returned to prominence when a video was posted to YouTube of a sighting of the creature in 2010 in Carbondale, Pennsylvania. Prior to the video, residents of the area had claimed to have seen the creature return. When a man heard unusual noises, he went to film it.

The general consensus of most Sasquatch experts is that this footage is a hoax. There are those who believe that the sighting could not possibly be faked with a simple costume or makeup. With the debate still raging on the Patterson-Gimlin film from 1967 in California, this debate will probably continue for some time as well.

There are reports of Sasquatch sightings throughout the Appalachians. The Bigfoot Research Organization is where you should report any sightings you might have yourself or encourage others to report if they haven't. It even allows older sightings to add to its database, so that the organization can chronicle encounters that may verify or corroborate other sightings.

In the town of Blue Ridge in North Georgia, you can visit Expedition Bigfoot. This museum is home to one of the largest collections of Sasquatch research in the world. There are casts of footprints, artifacts from expeditions and documents from every major sighting in history. The museum is a must stop for those who want to know more about the beasts known as Bigfoot.

PART VI
EERIE LOCATIONS

MAMMOTH CAVE

Cave City, Kentucky

Sprawling out under most of the Appalachians and beyond is the giant Mammoth Cave System. Some say that it should be known as the Eighth Natural Wonder of the World. Every weekend, more and more miles of the cave system are explored and are added to its mapped tunnel system. There is no telling how far they truly spread.

It is believed that the first humans to find these caves and use them as a respite from natural elements were from around twelve thousand years ago. There is archaeological evidence, including skeletal remains and petroglyphs, from four thousand years ago. One body was discovered in the cave that had been crushed by a boulder. He had a primitive digging tool next to his intact skull. Though not the first to find the cave, he would definitely be among its earliest explorers.

The Cherokees and Shawnees used the caves as shelter and even a base of operations during the French and Indian Wars of the mid-1700s. After they were removed from the area by post–Revolutionary War settlers, the main cave entrance was abandoned for a brief period.

In 1798, a two-hundred-acre claim from Valentine Simmons was the first public record of the main entrance to the cave. The great entrance was remarked on, but no one understood its true value until decades later. It passed through several hands until a merchant named Charles Wilkins

Mammoth Cave's main entrance into the miles of tunnels below has not changed in ages. *Photo by the author.*

realized that the cave was a natural mine for saltpeter, which could be used for gunpowder. Wilkins made a fortune on the backs of his slaves during the War of 1812 by selling his saltpeter to the military of the fledgling United States.

The cave soon became famous due to the saltpeter. Its reputation grew as Wilkins found several mummies distributed throughout the cave system. Tourists began to flock to the area, and Wilkins and his partner, Hyman Gratz, began to cash in by offering tours of the underground world they had been working. They used slaves and hired miners as tour guides.

In these early tours, many amateur spelunkers were killed. These tourists were walking on slick cave floors with only lanterns and torches for light. There are no official records of how many died, but there are locations in the caves where names were "smoked into the ceiling" with torches. These areas are still visible on today's much safer tours.

In 1838, Mammoth Cave passed into the hands of Franklin Gorin for $5,000. Gorin had a slave named Stephen Bishop whom he put to work mapping the caves. Bishop is now known to be the first person to have ever mapped the early days of the Mammoth Cave System. Gorin then built an inn and added roads and other modern conveniences for the time to improve tourism. More slaves were added to be guides.

The enslaved guides would work from 1839 until well into the 1870s. As they passed on, some had their children continue their work. Even the grandchildren of some of those original slave guides continued to host tours of the caves for more than one hundred years. The bodies of many of these guides are buried at the "Old Guides Cemetery" near the main entrance to the cave system.

In 1842, Dr. John Croghan had an idea that Mammoth Cave would be the perfect environment for the curing of tuberculosis. He turned a portion of the cave into a hospital ward and built several huts. He had the idea after hearing stories of how the slave guides never seemed to tire or get ill. He had heard stories of folks walking in the caves for hours and not tiring when they could barely walk a few feet above ground without extreme effort.

Sadly, the dampness of the caves and the darkness did little to improve the patients he brought there. If anything, they died even more quickly. The gaunt patients lost skin coloring, and their eyes would gloss over in

Inside Mammoth Cave lies Corpse Rock, where patients who succumbed to tuberculosis were laid before burial for visitors to see. *Image provided by Mammoth Cave National Park.*

the constant darkness. The rest of these poor, sick souls was also constantly interrupted as the tours continued through the ward into the cave.

As the patients began to die, they were laid out on a stone slab called "Corpse Rock." By 1849, even Croghan himself had died from the dreaded TB. He, too, was set atop Corpse Rock.

By the 1900s, more caves had been discovered nearby. Many tied into Mammoth Cave. Owners of Big Onyx Cave began a rivalry with other landowners with other entrances. Artifacts were stolen. Stories were fabricated in the press to downplay the claims of other caves. Court battles were numerous. Some battles were outright skirmishes between rival gangs of cave workers. Tourists still flocked to the caves.

In 1917, a man named Floyd Collins discovered a new cave that he called Crystal Cave. He continued to try to find new entrances to his spectacular cave that might be closer to roads to get those ever-important tourist dollars. On January 30, 1925, Floyd became trapped in a crawlspace more than fifty feet down. He called for help as best he could.

Collins became a news sensation on the new invention called radio. He was the first viral news story on the new media. People flocked from all over the world to see if they could help the intrepid spelunker. After two weeks, Collins died of exposure and dehydration—only three days before tunnellers reached his location. It took an additional two months to recover his body.

In 1926, a group of wealthy Kentuckians formed a committee to convert the region into a national park. This was going to be problematic, as many families lived in the lands needed and would not want to give up their homesteads. Many had been settled here since claiming the land after service in the Revolutionary War.

Some families did donate their lands. Thousands of people, however, were forcibly removed from the property via eminent domain. Many families still harbor strong grudges against the park. Many felt underpaid for their property. One owner was called away for an emergency, and by the time he returned, they had bulldozed his home. Resentment against the government is strong in this area for deeds such as this.

The caves themselves are a marvel to behold. There are numerous tours offered daily. More than 2 million visitors visit the park each year. Some of the tours are quite rigorous, but there are accessible tours for those with physical limitations.

Many of the caves are closed to the public due to White-Nose Syndrome, which affects much of the cave system's bat population. The little brown bat and the tricolored bat populations have declined nearly 90 percent in the caves in the decade since the disease was first discovered.

There are more than four hundred miles of caverns currently mapped, with more being added every single week. It is amazing to think how much more there could be down there to still be explored and charted.

Guides there have plenty of ghost stories. Some report seeing gaunt figures in the old TB huts that are still there. Others have claimed to have seen extra people in their tour groups that look out of time or in period clothing that vanish when approached. Most famously, people claim to hear Floyd Collins calling out for help near Crystal Cave.

Mammoth Cave is a must visit for anyone. There is just so much natural beauty and so much history to explore there. Simply remember to stay close to your guide. Book a tour ahead of time that you feel comfortable with. Do not forget to keep your eyes and ears open for the ghosts of past.

The Mushroom Mines

Lawton, Kentucky

Just outside Olive Hill, Kentucky, lies the remains of a town called Lawton. All that is left in the ghost town are some old structures that once housed a general store, a hotel and the offices of the Tygart Limestone Company. The source of all the jobs in the town of Lawton was the large underground mine, which now has more legends and true history far darker than its long-abandoned halls.

The Lawton Limestone Company was the original owner of the mountain. It was founded in 1910. The company shipped limestone rocks from a quarried ledge across the state to the Ashland Ironworks. As the open-pit mine began to produce less rock, it was decided to build an underground mine. The company became the Tygart Limestone Company in 1917 and soon began to dig.

The mine continued to grow, and more and more rock was being sent to ironworks everywhere and anywhere that needed stone thanks to the nearby Chesapeake & Ohio Railroad line. The mine grew and quickly spanned hundreds of thousands of square feet. By the time it closed just after World War II, the mines had incorporated more than 136 acres and 2.6 million miles of tunnels.

The tunnels sat abandoned after the closure of the company. The town of Lawton dried up. The nearby town of Olive Hill was where the trains and

The entrance to the Mushroom Mines. *Photo by the author.*

roads now served. Even when the work dried up at the mines, there were those who wondered, "What will they do with the mine itself?"

Some farmers came up with a brilliant idea for the place. The mines would have an ideal temperature and humidity level to grow and can mushrooms. Plus, it was still only a short distance to the roads and railroad. There were also plenty of nearby farms that could help supply fertilizer and other needed materials.

It was a moderate success. By June 1968, the first crop had been planted. The mine sent out its first canned shipment on Christmas Eve of that same year. During this period, the mine floors were leveled, and some entrances were sealed. Vents were added for shipping and canning facilities. By the mid-1970s, they were shipping millions of pounds of mushrooms yearly.

Eventually, even this business died out. The overhead of the mines simply did not match the profits needed to sustain operations. The mines shipped their last mushrooms in the early 1980s, barely into their second decade of operations. The mines sat abandoned for a long time after this.

Locals would use the mines as a place to get away from it all. It was a rite of passage for teenagers to spend the night in the creepy old mine. People would see how much they could explore. A well-known pond inside became a popular camping spot due to the access to the fresh water.

During this period, stories began to be told of monsters and ghosts in the long, dark tunnels. The unearthly quiet of the mine would echo any strange noise to add to the ambience of terror. There were frequent reports of slaughtered animals found within the caves by would-be explorers, which led to stories of cult activity within the mines.

On February 7, 2004, the bodies of a missing couple from the county were found deep inside the mine. An anonymous tip had sent the police to find the corpses of Gary and Cheryl Young in a shallow grave. It was discovered that they had been murdered by their own son, Andrew. His girlfriend, Stephanie Griffith, was also implicated in the crime.

Locals were not surprised to find bodies in the mine, as criminal activity had been happening there for years. What police officer would patrol miles and miles of old abandoned tunnels? Reports of drug deals, prostitution, human trafficking and even a satanic cult surrounded the areas of the "Mushroom Mines."

One local told us of going to the mines one night in June 2005. She had decided to camp by the small pond that lies about a quarter mile within the tunnels. She was there with her boyfriend and another couple. They had brought enough supplies to stay for a few nights in the dark underworld of the caves. Late that night, they were awoken by the sound of someone throwing rocks at them in the darkness. Their lanterns could not find who was doing this.

The next day, they moved their campsite closer to the exit after being unnerved the night before. They were bedding down again for the following evening when a large car drove into the mine and almost ran them over. The driver apologized for the near mishap. He quizzed them about why they were staying there. He asked if they had hunted out the lake. He also asked if they knew about the bodies that had been found there.

The man drove off into the tunnels, and they could hear the engine and tires long after it had driven into the darkness within. That was enough for the campers. They packed up and left in a hurry.

After returning to town, they realized that they had left an important item back at the campsite in the mine, so they returned to the hill. As they drove up, they saw the strange car parked outside the mine. A group of people clad in dark robes were marching into the mine in a single-file line. They decided that the important item was not that important after all and left, never to return.

In 2006, the mine was sold to a Silicon Valley data storage company, Global Data. It felt that the mines were well worth the $1 million price tag. It intended to create the Stone Mountain Ultra-Secure Data Complex and create thousands of needed jobs for the area.

It was all a complex fraud scheme unfortunately, even though several buildings were constructed. The mayor of nearby Olive Hill had been hired on to be a project manager. Global Data, the California company behind it all, filed for bankruptcy to avoid payments. Many of the construction crews were unpaid for months of work. The owner of Global Data was arrested for dozens of accounts of fraud.

The land's deed went into trust, and it took a years before the title could be cleared. It is now owned by a man in Maryland, who is wanting to sell what he refers to as "Mega Mountain" for a great deal at $7 million. It would be just over one nickel per cubic foot for the tunnels. The owner still hopes to see it become a high-tech facility or even an entertainment complex. Who knows what the future will bring for the Mushroom Mines?

Today, you can still visit the ghost town remains of Lawton just outside Olive Hill. You can drive up the road to view the two entrances to the mine. The land is private property and is not open to tourists or investigation without proper permission from the owner. Proof of insurance will be required, as well as a liability release, if you would like to venture into the dark of the earth legally at the time of this writing in late 2021. Hopefully someone will buy the mine and put the sixty acres of tunnels to good use.

The Appalachians are full of mines that offer tours and even paranormal excursions. Check with the local tourism boards in any area to find ones open to visitors.

WRIGHT-PATTERSON AIR FORCE BASE

Dayton, Ohio

The oldest flying fields in the world are found at Wright-Patterson Air Force Base. In the lands just outside Dayton, Ohio, Wilbur and Orville Wright began their early tests and experiments with heavier-than-air flight. Admittedly, their first successful flight was on a test trip at Kill Devil Hills in Kitty Hawk, North Carolina, but that site is not an airfield. The Wrights used what was called Huffman Field to further develop their planes.

Just prior to 1910, the brothers bought Huffman Field and used it for their flying school for new pilots. One of their earliest graduates was First Lieutenant "Hap" Arnold. Hap would later become a five-star general. He was the commander of the U.S. Army Air Forces in World War II and the first general ever of the U.S. Air Force.

The school closed in 1916. In 1917, the United States entered into World War I. The army purchased Huffman Field, an area next to it that the

Wright-Patterson Air Force Base from the air. Given the sheer size of all the fields, it would be easy to hide a secret project here. *Image provided by the U.S. Air Force National Archive.*

Wrights had named Wright Field and another area named McCook Field. Dayton housed America's greatest concentration of flying experts due to the Wright school. The military took advantage of it and began its early exploration into the potential military use of aeroplanes.

After the end of World War I, the three fields—Wright, Huffman and McCook—became the focal point for the military's use of aviation. In 1918, the army established the U.S. Army Air Services, using lessons learned from European air services in the war. President Woodrow Wilson signed the act creating the new service branch.

Planes built prior to the war were barely more than gliders and were not practical for military or commercial use. During the war, technology advanced quite a bit, and the planes being made in the area were getting much better. All that early testing took place at these fields.

In the 1920s, it was determined that McCook Field was too confined for the new, more modern planes that could now reach one hundred miles per hour and could fly for hundreds of miles. The original Wright Field merged with an army facility called the Fairfield Depot. The entire military base was then renamed Wright Field to honor the original brothers.

Before World War II, the area became a hub for research and development for all military aircraft. Biplanes changed to monoplane aircraft. Engine and material improvements were always on the cutting edge at Wright Field.

World War II caused the size of Wright Field to explode with growth. The population went from under four thousand to well over fifty thousand airmen and staff in a very short period. All sorts of buildings were thrown up in a great hurry. Housing, admin buildings, recreational centers, test facilities and, of course, hangars. Around the base, the factories around Dayton went into overdrive to meet demands of the war effort.

In 1947, the air force was finally separated from the army. In 1948, Wright AFB merged with Patterson Air Field. The new base was named Wright-Patterson Air Force Base. It would be the heart of military technical advancement for years to come. Every U.S. military conflict since has relied on technology and support from Wright-Patterson.

Shortly after the famous Roswell crash and in response to several other sightings of UFOs across the United States, the air force began a program call Operation Sign. It was housed at Wright-Patterson. Later, a more public version would begin called Project Blue Book. It was also operated out of Wright-Patterson AFB.

Project Blue Book would run for more than seventeen years and would document more than twelve thousand cases of potential UFO encounters. Not all were investigated thoroughly. Many were given little more than a cursory case study. After a few condemning reports, notably the Condon Report, it was determined that UFOs were not a significant threat to the United States. So, the funding was pulled, and Project Blue Book was closed in 1969. While not firmly concluding there were *no* aliens, it was more concerned about the rising threats of the USSR and China.

Now, many say that this is the end of the alien connections with WPAFB. There are numerous parties, however, who believe otherwise. Researchers claim that the Blue Book was merely a smokescreen to hide real investigations into captured alien technology. Many more have come forward over the years, saying that Wright-Patterson has been home to alien technology as far back as the 1947 Roswell incident.

The U.S. Air Force denies all of this. However, it has, over the course of the years, changed its cover stories of Roswell from weather balloon to secret balloon project that would spy on Russian nuclear tests. The air force even changed some of the early reports of Project Blue Book after declassification in recent years. Therefore, many UFO researchers dismiss many government reports, as they never seem to be truly definitive.

An abundance of reports came out from former military personnel detailing crashed extra-terrestrial craft being tested and reverse engineered at Wright-Patterson. Albert Einstein's assistant even claimed to have been flown there with the noted scientist to look at a strange "grey-colored alien being." Several people have come forward claiming that there are at least two saucer-like craft and two alien bodies stored at the facility.

Most of these claims are well documented, and the location is noted as a secret Hangar 18. There was even a movie about the very subject released in 1980. The existence of Hangar 18 is widely disputed, as there is no Hangar 18 at Wright-Patterson AFB. There is a Building 18, which appears to be a very nondescript office facility. There are rumors of underground facilities at the field, but most have been disproven.

With all of that said, there does seem to be a large number of witnesses and discussions. In 2019, a former air force major claimed in a book that in 1978 the air force had shot down and killed an alien near Fort Dix in New Jersey.

Just before dawn on January 18, 1978, there was a string of sightings of unidentified craft flying over the northern Appalachians toward Fort Dix and nearby McGuire Air Force Base. After being on alert for the morning, a military police officer on guard at the rear of McGuire AFB was ordered to allow New Jersey State Police onto the base through his entrance gate.

When the troopers arrived, they told the airman that a Fort Dix MP had been in pursuit of a low-flying UFO. One of the troopers told him that someone suddenly jumped in front of the MP's car, and he opened fire on

Wright-Patterson Air Force Base has no Hangar 18, but it does have this, the nondescript Building 18. Is it a clever front? *Photo by the author.*

Illustrations of alien bodies as described by witnesses that are allegedly being stored and studied at Wright-Patterson Air Force Base. *Illustration by Kari Schultz.*

it. The intruder was supposedly very small and slender, with an unusually large head. It was wounded by the MP and had jumped the fence between the bases—thus the need to get into McGuire.

The airman said that he went with the troopers and found the strange body lying on a deserted runway at the back of the base. The police roped off the crime scene. Within minutes, some soldiers came in wearing blue berets and a uniform unfamiliar to the MP. They assumed command of the investigation and even sent the police away with minimal discussion.

The MP claimed that he was told to not discuss the incident, as it was top secret and he would be court-martialed if he did. The other guards at his post were also similarly warned. He later learned that the unknown soldiers had flown in on a plane from Wright-Patterson AFB and had taken the mysterious body away in a crate on the same cargo plane they had come in on.

A few days after the incident, the MP and others from Fort Dix were taken to Wright-Patterson in Ohio. There they were interrogated and warned not to speak of the incident. They all were forced to sign forms that were binding for life, according to the MP.

In recent years, those involved have begun to come forward about the Fort Dix/McGuire incident. All described the body as a short and slender alien with no clothing. It had an enlarged head and only three long, thin fingers and three squat toes. One airman said that the feet almost looked like those of an ape, but the body was no ape.

The major was in command of the officers involved. The men told him these accounts. Their claims have been backed up by several more witnesses coming forward in the past few years since word of him going public has come out. Many of the names of those involved are still being withheld. The air force has denied the incident and the claims of yet another body being sent to the base. The flight logs from both Wright-Patterson and McGuire bases for this day are not available through the Freedom of Information Act, for reasons unknown.

To this day, Wright-Patterson Air Force Base holds a very strong strategic footprint for the U.S. Air Force. It is a technological powerhouse, always at the forefront of future technology testing. Is it any wonder that many consider it the real Area 51? Although it is not in the Appalachians, many consider this base to be the reason so many UFOs and so much other unusual activity are spread so close in nearby West Virginia, Eastern Kentucky and the other surrounding states.

CONCLUSION

The stories here are by no means a definitive list of all the strange and unusual things the Appalachians have to offer. This is but a grand overview of some of the highlights. We hope you found some of these tales inspiring for road trips. Maybe you will investigate the history behind some of these stories a bit more.

While many of the strange and unusual stories within defy logic or reason, most echo the legends and lore of our immigrant ancestors. Many were passed down from Native American cultures long lost. They all get stirred up in our melting pot like a great bubbling cauldron and come out as something new.

The Appalachians are the oldest mountains in the world. If not for some ancient geological changes, they would stretch from Iceland to Mississippi. It is interesting to note that the Scottish Highlands were once a part of this majestic mountain range. The areas we visit in this book are merely a fraction of the ground we could cover.

We were told some of the holler monster stories in strict confidence. There are so many more I wish I could share—the Lorelei, the Huntington Hobgoblin, the Judas Coin, the Ghost of the Moon Man, the One-Thousand-Year Fire of Centralia and even another "Screaming Jenny," as well as so many more ghost stories it would make your hair curl. Those will have wait for future volumes after much more research and many more trips are completed.

While it is easy to dismiss the wild strangeness of some of these tales, it is also easy to see the truth in many of them. Most tales are told to warn us about common threats. Stay away from that cave: it is dangerous. Stay clear of that place: someone was murdered there and now it is haunted. Do not talk to strangers, as they might be a devil in disguise. All are good points to know.

The famous Bigfoot butt print at Expedition Bigfoot in Blue Ridge, Georgia. *Photo by the author.*

We will never know the answers to some of the questions brought up by these areas of research. Is Bigfoot real? To some, it is only a matter of time before we prove he is. Are UFOs real? Only a year ago, the answer would have been a solid no from anyone in the government. Now new government teams are being formed to investigate what are now called Unidentified Aerial Phenomena (UAP). Is Indrid Cold working for them? Well, I doubt we will ever know the answer to that one.

We are incredibly grateful to have had the assistance of so many researchers who have come before us. We actively sought out local sources on our travels to each location in the book. So many historical societies, libraries, paranormal investigative groups and cryptid hunters opened their resources to us.

When the global pandemic shut everything down just as we were ramping up for our first major research and photo gathering trips, we thought that was the end of this book for some time. Thankfully, we were able to virtually meet with many more people and continue our work on this project. The photos and research trips simply had to wait a little while.

Before we go, we have a couple stories in the appendices after this. The first is a Florida encounter that ties into a particularly important part of this book. It is the very reason this book exists. We wrote a little about it in our chapter on Indrid Cold early in this book, but we felt it was necessary to see just how far the weirdness of Appalachia ties into so much everywhere else. The final part of this book is Mark's own holler monster encounter. This is a very personal story for him and one he is happy to share with you. He hopes you enjoy his monster story by the campfire.

Lastly, we would like to say that, usually, the most common question we get is: "Where is the scariest place in all of your travels?" That is a tough question to answer. There are places where truly dark things have happened.

Netherworld is the apex of haunted houses in America. The Netherspawn are waiting for you every Halloween at Stone Mountain, Georgia! *Photo by the author.*

There are places that just felt wrong. There are places where we really did feel the presence of something beyond our understanding.

"What type of scary?" is often our reply.

They usually say, "I want to go someplace where I can get scared."

We tell them that that is an easy question to answer. There is one place at the base of Stone Mountain in Georgia where we can safely assure you that you will feel scared and overwhelmed. Netherworld is a haunted attraction that is so amazing that words do not do it justice. The sheer level of detail will astound you. You really do feel like you have gone into another world of horror. Do not miss it! It is like going to the Disney World of scary places.

If you decide to visit some of the locations described in this book, make sure to stay safe and have a great time. Call ahead to most places, as many are seasonal or have limited capacity for visitors. The more rural locations may require some extra preparation. Any private locations that are not open to visitors we intentionally kept vague in the book. Most, though, are easily found with an internet search or two.

Please feel free to drop us a line at our website, EerieTravels.com, to tell us of anything you feel we need to cover or simply to tell us what you think. You can find our older books at EerieFlorida.com. We would love to hear about your own holler monster or family ghost story or if you had an experience at any of the locations we mentioned.

THE CRESTVIEW INCIDENT

INDRID COLD IN FLORIDA

Miami, Florida

> *I half thought about not putting this in the book at all. I was researching this strange event in Florida and the huge UFO flap in the early 1950s. This was going to be the basis for my next book in our "Eerie Florida" book line. As we researched the Crestview Sighting and started interviewing witness that were willing to talk, one name came at us out of the blue, and it is the basis for this whole book. I decided it would be an injustice not to include what started us on the road to Appalachia without it.*
> *—Mark Muncy*

After the success of *Eerie Florida*, I found myself getting frequent letters and e-mails of strange encounters with unusual things all throughout Florida. I frequently received e-mails from witness of a strange event in 1967 near Miami. I obtained this account from one witness to the incident:

> *I was in the 6th grade at Crestview Elementary School, in Miami. During recess in April 1967, I and hundreds of other students from Crestview and a few teachers, witnessed 3 oval shaped objects coming through a few clouds, on a mostly a clear day, directly over our heads. My teacher gathered our class into a line. We watched as the two smaller of the three oval objects, appeared to be dancing around the larger oval shaped object coming down towards us. The larger object, seemed to be the size of a cruise ship,*

but its shape was oval, and cigar shaped. It was shiny and metal like. I saw the large object land in the field near our school. I didn't see where the other two objects went.

What seemed like hours before long, we were told to go home. I was one of the students who rode our bikes to the landing area not far from our school. We stepped over a berm and found a field of weeds and grass that appeared to be charred and smashed into an oval shape and seemed to be the size of a large boat. There was no object there, but the remains of something that had recently been lying there.

Before long, men in uniforms and news press started to interview us kids. I listened to a boy who had the same accounting as me. The following day, the Miami Herald *told the story and said that it was helicopters on maneuvers from the nearby Homestead Air Force Base. I knew otherwise and understand now that they had to state that to avoid mass hysteria.*

In the years to follow, I took my children to the sighting location, as they had heard my accounting for many years. This was in the '90s and we found that in the same location, as where I saw the UFO land, was now the location of the Miami Football Stadium (off Miami Gardens Drive and 183rd Street). It had been built, after they closed the Orange Bowl Football Stadium. The stadium amazingly stands in the very sight where I saw UFO land and come to think of it, the UFO was about the size of the stadium floor!

I made a few arrangements to talk with several of the witnesses. There were lots of stories of UFO encounters throughout the state, and this one held particular interest for me. The government involvement made it stand out to me. One of the witnesses told me that he had been interviewed after school just after the incident. His father had a list of the names of the men who had interviewed him.

The list of names was a prize I could not believe. I would have names of officers I could trace. I would most likely not be able to track the officers down, but I might at least be able to get some Freedom of Information Act papers filed. To say I was excited was an incredible understatement. I had no idea of the shock that awaited me.

The list was in an old handwritten phone address book. The pages were slightly yellowed. The witness was a child at the time and now holds a public office in the area so does not want to come forward just yet. He figures that when he retires in a few more years, he will come forward. He did allow me to discuss the names.

"10 Chaotic Minutes" read the headlines from the *Crestview Sighting*. Later reports would claim that it was only helicopters on maneuvers. The witnesses say otherwise. *Reprinted with permission from the* Miami Herald, *April 1967.*

The first two names on the paper were short and simple: Lieutenant Sinclair from the U.S. Air Force and Captain Smith from the U.S. Coast Guard. Neither name would be easy to research, but it would not be impossible. I froze in place when I read the third name: "Cold. Government Man."

When the witness saw my face, he asked if I was okay. I asked him if he remembered the "Government Man." He said he did not say much during the questions. He simply smiled a lot and wore a very shiny suit.

I finished my interview with the witness and told him to hang on to that book forever. I explained to him, "When you are ready to come forward, that page is going to be invaluable to researchers." He asked why. I had to tell him the tale of Indrid Cold from West Virginia.

Driving home from southeast Florida seemed like the longest ride of my life. This was huge. Did Indrid Cold suddenly start working for the government? Was he really one of the Men in Black? Why was I suddenly being drawn back to the myths and legends of my youth in the heart of the Appalachians? The road called, and I had to follow.

There is so much more to Crestview, but that's for a different book at a later time. I began to research Indrid Cold in earnest. Freedom of Information, of course, left me with nothing. So much research and digging had been done on Cold over the years that there would be no stone left unturned on him. However, none of those researchers had any knowledge that he might have been involved with a government agency after his initial sightings.

THE BENCH LEG
OF GOEBLE RIDGE

LOUISA, KENTUCKY

I had heard stories of the beast that lurked near my family's lands in Kentucky. My father used to tell me the story of the creature with the dumbest name I'd ever heard that hunted the woods of Goble Ridge in Eastern Kentucky.

We only lived a few hours away in Ohio, so we used to spend weekends "roughing it" in Louisa, and my uncle or my dad would tell us of the "Bench Leg of Goeble Ridge." All of us kids would laugh at the name, me especially. Now, I had already had some encounters with ghostly phenomena and other unexplainable experiences. For some reason, I just never believed in the local legendary beast…until I saw it.

Any kid who grew up anywhere near Isaac Church can tell you the legend of the creature. The story goes that an old peddler in the late 1700s would have his cart pulled by an ox out along what was then known as Muncy Meeks Road. He would sell pots, pans and other odds and ends to the scattered farms along the ridge. The families all knew that he was coming from the sound of the old cow bell and the rattle of his wagon.

The story goes that some nefarious types figured he'd have some quick cash on him and possibly gold or silver, so they set up an ambush under an old tree at a bend in the road where they could hide behind the ridge. Then they robbed the peddler. He resisted by breaking off a limb from the tree and using it as a club. They overpowered him and killed him. To hide the

The Bench Leg Monster of the back hills of eastern Kentucky. *Illustration by Kari Schultz.*

murder, they butchered the ox and buried the whole mess in a shallow grave under the old tree.

As many times as I've heard the tale, up to that point it never changes. It's afterward that everyone tells it differently, depending on which of the several families in the area tell the tale. Cyrus descendants say that the peddler was of Romani heritage and that a powerful curse brought forth a beast like a big cat that walks on two legs and carries the old peddler's club to take vengeance on the highwaymen. Meeks family members say that the old peddler's wife was a witch who animated the bones of her husband and the cow into some odd undead creature that hunts Kentucky lands to keep away bad people. The Isaac clan generally just says that it was divine vengeance that killed all the wrongdoers.

My dad told it differently. The Muncy family owns most of the land the creature is said to live on. Each generation seems to have some odd encounter or tale of the "Bench Leg." Heck, the old tree in the legend is supposed to be the creepy old tree that is right across the street from where we "rough it" in our trailer. No other trees will grow in the immediate area around it. The stories tend to be shared alongside the big fire pit, where we can stay up late telling ghost stories (basic cable sucked after 11:00 p.m. in the mid-1980s). Almost every member of our family has seen the beast, including my dad, his brother and me.

My dad told me that he saw it once when he was very young while out walking his old herd of cattle back. He was walking in the holler when he saw an extra head of cattle. It seemed a little small, with an odd glow about its head. My dad called to his brother and told him that one of the cows must have foaled without their knowledge. He got his brother to try to corner the new calf by going around one side of a small copse of trees as my dad came from the other side. They blinked in astonishment as the beast vanished in front of their eyes. My dad said that just before it vanished, he could have sworn that it turned and looked at him with a glowing human head.

I know it's not terrifying. I know it's just odd. I also know that my father never lied about a thing in his life, so I know he honestly believed every word of his story. My uncle also talked about the incident in hushed tones; if you knew my uncle, you would know that happened very rarely while he was alive.

My incident came many years later. I used to drag some of my city friends with me to our land in Kentucky nearly weekly just to have someone to goof off or go hunting with. We found and cleaned out my parents' old Airstream trailer, killed all the spiders and snakes that had nested in it and dragged it down to the edge of an old baseball field my grandparents used to have on their land.

There wasn't a ball field there anymore. It was simply a baseball diamond–sized clearing in a pristine wilderness. All we really cared about was that it was about a half mile away from where the grownups spent their time, so we could talk about girls, school and our parents and tell *really* scary ghost stories—not ones about a dumb cow-monster with man's head and a possible wooden leg.

One night, just after we had gotten to a shaky sleep after a particularly scary retelling of the "Haunting of Hill House" by yours truly to my friends, one of the horses that occasionally grazed in the area got really close to one of our windows and snorted…loudly. You would have thought the devil himself was at our door, as the three early teenage boys ran out of that trailer with bats and bb guns at the ready to slay whatever beast had awakened us.

I seriously think we made the horse's night, as I imagine the sight when we all realized what fell beast had disturbed our slumber. We all laughed pretty hard.

That's when we heard the sound of more hooves. Was there a second horse out grazing that we hadn't heard about? Was this some echo from a nearby farm? We all got quiet. That's when I saw the glow through the tree line. I can still feel the hairs on the back of my neck stand on end as I type these words even now more than thirty years later.

The eerie green light was coming right for us, and I knew exactly what it was. I was about to have my own story to add to our family's litany. It burst forth, and I could see that it was about the size of a big cat of some sort. It had a deep black fur all over it, and the moonlight seemed to sink into it. I would compare it to a large panther except that it had no tail. I swear it had hooves and not claws, and its head was a misshapen thing that looked like pictures I'd seen of the Elephant Man. I thought to myself, "It does have the head of a man, but he was one ugly sonofabitch." I vaguely remember trying to see if it did have a wooden leg.

It made a quick turn and ran into the deeper woods just behind our little trailer. My memory is foggy after the incident. Adrenaline was leaving quickly. I recall the horse bolting toward third base and the pond in that area. My friends all scattered and ran for the big trailer. I could hear them yelling for me to "Get the ---- out of there!" I don't remember running, but I do remember being out of breath as I collapsed on the couch in the big trailer up the hill. I can still see my friend PJ yelling, "What the ---- was that?"

The Bench Leg tree on Isaac Park Road. *Photo by the author.*

My dad came out of his room with mom in tow behind him, although it had to be two or three o'clock in the morning. He had drawn his revolver and was heading for the shotgun cabinet. I'm certain that he intended to kill whatever had scared his boy and his friends.

From our inability to articulate thanks to sheer terror and a half-mile sprint, he thought we had a bear or some sort of cougar loose in the area. Then our eyes made contact. He put his gun down and took a deep breath. He knew what had happened.

I don't 100% percent know what it was. I've never seen it since. The encounter makes zero sense to me. We weren't in any apparent danger. Apart from the legends of the Bench Leg beating up bad people and seeking revenge on the highwaymen, I don't think I've ever heard of anyone actually being hurt by the creature.

I could speculate as to what it is. I could make a more reasonable story as to what happened that night—make it more interesting and even add to the legend. I could do all that, I guess. All I know is that I now have a tale to add to the late-night fires on Goeble Ridge.

Mark Muncy and Kari Schultz with one of their pet spiders that they originally found under a burned-out barn in New York. (Truthfully, it's a wonderful prop showcased at Netherworld in Stone Mountain, Georgia.) *Author's photo.*

ABOUT THE AUTHOR AND ILLUSTRATOR

MARK MUNCY is an author of horror and science fiction. He has spent more than three decades collecting ghostly tales and reports of legendary beasts. He has previously written three books for The History Press, including *Creepy Florida*, *Eerie Florida*, and *Freaky Florida*. He is a frequent guest on *Coast-to-Coast AM*, *NerdTalk Live*, *Drinking with Authors* and *Into the Fray Radio*. He is a commentator and collaborator on numerous programs, including *Expedition X*, *Sasquatch Chronicles*, *Road Trips with Ripley's* and many more TV and radio shows. He can also be found hosting his online show "Eerie Travels." He lives in St. Petersburg, Florida, on the remains of an ancient shell midden with his wife, Kari Schultz. Occasionally, he is visited by his children when they remember he is still there. You can find out more at www.eerieflorida.com.

KARI SCHULTZ is an illustrator at Fox Dream Studio who enjoys drawing cute and creepy creatures. She has been working on art as long as she can remember and reading folklore and horror almost as long. She has illustrated several books of legends and monsters for The History Press, including *Eerie Florida*, *Eerie Alabama*, *Eerie New Mexico*, *Creepy Florida* and *Freaky Florida*. She has a thing for foxes. When not drawing, she is the caretaker of her baby dragon named Clawdius and her pythons Missy, Pajamas and Thulsa Doom. She also raises jumping spiders and tarantulas. She can be lured forth from her home with poke bowls or pasta.

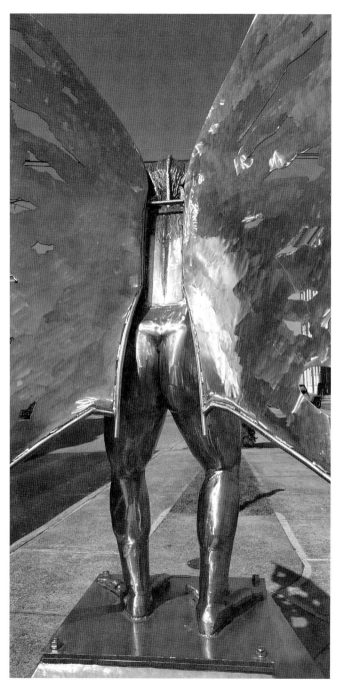

The Mothman statue's famous shiny posterior. The End! *Photo by the author.*

Visit us at
www.historypress.com